Visual Sources Series

NORMAN ENGLAND

Peter Lane

Formerly Principal Lecturer in History
Coloma College of Education, Kent

B.T. BATSFORD LTD London

First published 1980
© Peter Lane 1980

ISBN 0 7134 3356

Printed in Great Britain by
The Anchor Press Ltd, Tiptree, Essex
for the Publishers B.T. Batsford Ltd,
4 Fitzhardinge Street, London W1H 0AH

For Christopher Dominic to mark his
first year in the classroom

Acknowledgment

The Author and Publishers thank the following for their kind permission to reproduce copyright illustrations: Aerofilms Ltd for figs 14, 23, 69, 71 and 74; the British Library for fig
54; and Trustees of the British Museum for figs 25, 28, 34, 64 and 80; the British Tourist
Authority for fig 24; the Cambridge University Collection (Crown Copyright) for fig 5; John
R. Freeman for figs 3, 20, 21, 22, 31, 43, 45, 47, 50, 62, 79, 82 and 83; the Honourable
Company of Grocers for fig 44; A.F. Kersting for figs 26, 53, 61 and 63; Quentin Lloyd for
fig 32; the Mansell Collection for figs 19, 57 and 59; the National Monuments Record for
figs 55, 70 and 73; the National Museum of Wales for fig 48; the Public Record Office,
London for fig 18: Radio Times Hulton Picture Library for figs 2, 6, 7, 8, 9, 10, 12, 13, 17,
27, 36, 37, 38, 39, 41, 49, 51, 52, 56, 60, 65, 85, 89 and 92; Kenneth Scowen for fig 58;
Edwin Smith for fig 72; the University Library, Newcastle-upon-Tyne for fig 40. The other
illustrations appearing in the book are the property of the Publishers.

Contents

Acknowledgment   2

List of Illustrations   4

Introduction   5

1 England before the Conquest 1042-1066   7

2 The Battle of Hastings and the Conquest of England   13

3 A New and Stronger Monarchy   20

4 The Barons and their Castles   28

5 The Knights and their Manors   35

6 Farming   41

7 Towns and Townspeople   47

8 Home Life   54

9 Trade — Inland and Overseas   61

10 The Church   67

11 Monks and Monasteries   74

12 Norman Warfare   82

13 Entertainment   87

Other Visual Aids   94

Index   95

The Illustrations

1	Edward the Confessor and Harold	7
2	Harold enters Bosham church	8
3	The King with his ministers	8
4	A primitive plough	9
5	Open fields at Laxton, Notts	10
6	Edward the Confessor's funeral	11
7	Coronation of Harold	11
8	Harold's oath and his return to England	11
9	The comet	13
10	William's fleet	14
11	A knight gets into his armour	14
12	Building the castle at Hastings	14
13	Harold's death at Hastings	15
14	The Tower of London, aerial view	16
15	Part of Offa's Dyke	17
16	Map of castles, royal dwellings and forests	21
17	William and his guests at table	21
18	Domesday Book	23
19	Taking an oath	24
20	Henry I crosses English Channel	25
21	The marriage of Matilda	26
22	A prisoner in the Tower of London	28
23	Castle Rising, Norfolk	29
24	Pembroke Castle	29
25	Curtained beds for the rich	31
26	Castle Hedingham, Essex	31
27	A royal banquet	32
28	Hawking	33
29	The manor at Boarstall, Bucks	35
30	A plough and a harrow	35
31	A reeve supervises reaping	37
32	Godmersham barn	37
33	Bathing a child in a cooking pot	38
34	Fishing	39
35	Open fields at Braunton, Devon	41
36	A four-oxen plough	41
37	Breaking up the soil with hammers	42
38	Haymaking	44
39	Sheep-shearing	44
40	Reaping barley	45
41	Threshing	45
42	Plan of Norwich	48
43	Plan of London	48
44	Coat of arms of the Company of Grocers	50
45	A guild officer examining work of apprentice and craftsman	50
46	Selling fish	50
47	Collecting water	52
48	Interior of a cruck house	54
49	Harold upstairs	55
50	A man by an open fire	55
51	Cooking over an open fire	57
52	Feeding the chickens	57
53	The Jew's House, Lincoln	57
54	Spinning wool	59
55	Small fishing boats	61
56	Travelling on rough roads	61
57	A cobbler's workshop	62
58	The old market hall, Chipping Campden	63
59	Collecting market tolls	65
60	London Bridge	65
61	Durham Cathedral nave	68
62	Plan of Canterbury	69
63	St. Peter and his keys	69
64	Devils dressed as women	72
65	Carving of bear-baiting	72
66	Font, Castle Frome	72
67	Pilgrim's badge of St. Thomas	73
68	Map of dioceses and monasteries, 1035	74
69	Rievaulx Abbey	74
70	Ground plan of Fountains Abbey	76
71	Fountains Abbey remains	76
72	*Lavatorium*, Gloucester	76
73	Chester Cathedral	77
74	Worcester Cathedral	77
75	The scribe Eadwine	79
76	Medieval builders	79
77	Battle scene	82
78	A castle under siege	82
79	Stephen	83
80	Armourers	83
81	Knight of a Crusade	83
82	A knight unseated	85
83	Knights in a mock fight	87
84	Practising with the quintain	87
85	Hunting	87
86	Return from the hunt	88
87	Inside the great hall, Moat House, Kent	88
88	A minstrel	90
89	Archery	90
90	Coventry Miracle Play	92
91	A game of cricket	92
92	Trap-ball	92

Introduction

How can we discover what life was like in the past? What evidence is available for historians to examine? Historians studying modern as opposed to ancient history can turn to written or printed material. For instance, the diaries of Samuel Pepys will aid their study of the seventeenth century and the Reports of the Royal Commissions on factory conditions will tell them of the nineteenth century. Many such documents have been published and can be used by young historians who need no longer rely simply on the text book for ideas of what life was like in 1300, 1500 or 1700. Collections of published documents on Norman England are also available. I have used some of these documents in this book. If you wish to read more, I suggest that you look at some of the following:

W.O. Hassall *How They Lived 55BC-1485AD* (Basil Blackwell, Oxford, 1962)

W.O. Hassall *They Saw it Happen 55BC-1485AD* (Basil Blackwell, Oxford, 1962)

A.F. Scott *Everyone a Witness: The Norman Age* (White Lion Publishers)

Some of the documents are very long and difficult to understand. Some are translations of quite complicated poems or long accounts of battles. Many of us are unable or unwilling to use them. With illustrated material, on the other hand, it is quite different. Illustrations mean something to us straight away. If we look at the origins of the Shelter housing campaign in Britain we can see how pictures spoke louder than words. Many official reports on the problem of housing in modern Britain had been printed and might have been read. But it was only after the BBC had shown the television play *Cathy Come Home* about a homeless young mother that the plight of the homeless was really brought home to everybody. On the very day after they had seen the play a group of young people decided to do something about the problem, and Shelter was born. The visual evidence had made much more impact than the written word.

The same is true in the study of history. We can, of course, study history through the written document, but we may understand it better if we examine the evidence of illustrations. For example, we may get a better idea of the Battle of Hastings by examining the pictures of it in the Bayeux Tapestry than by reading about it. The back-breaking boredom of the life of the Norman peasant can be described in words, but this life may be more vividly shown in pictures of ploughing, harrowing and clod-breaking.

At the end of each chapter I have suggested a number of questions which the student might tackle. I hope that they will help to show how the historian works. There are questions which will bring out the importance of the evidence presented; there are some which ask the young historian to compare one piece of evidence with another; and there are some which ask the young historian to use his imagination as the more senior historians have to do.

I have offered the young historians a variety of work — painting, letter-writing, the composition of a frieze, and so on. The questions and assignments are not meant to be a final, complete list of all the work that might be done. There are many more questions to be asked about the pictures, and many other kinds of work that might be tackled. I hope that what there is will help the young historian to get a clear idea of what Norman England was like — and lead to further reading and research.

1 England before the Conquest 1042-1066

1 Edward the Confessor, King of England from 1042 to 1066, can be seen sitting on his throne in his palace at Westminster in this section of the Bayeux Tapestry. The word *"Rex"* with his name is Latin for King. Edward is talking to Harold who was about to set off for France.

Edward the Confessor (*pic. 1*)
Before coming to the English throne in 1042 Edward had lived in Normandy in France. His father, Ethelred the Unready, was English, but his mother, Emma, was French — a daughter of the Duke of Normandy. Edward liked the Norman people and admired their way of life. When he came to the throne of England he brought some Normans with him and he continued to follow many Norman practices — in language and in building, for example. In particular, he had been devoted to the Church in Normandy, and in England he kept up his support for the Church. He was always pleased when Normans came across the Channel to visit him. One of the most popular of these visitors was William, the Duke (or ruler) of Normandy.

Edward, the Normans and the Saxons
When he became King, Edward had to contend with some very powerful Saxon nobles who held places in the State and the Church. The leader of the Saxon nobles was Earl Godwin. Edward married Godwin's daughter, Edith, and this marriage strengthened the influence that Godwin had over Edward.

When Godwin died he was succeeded as leader of the Saxon nobles by his son, Harold Godwinson.

At the same time, however, Edward brought in Norman advisers. One became Archbishop of Canterbury, the leader of the Church in England. Norman abbots were put in charge of important monasteries (Chapter 11). There were also Norman landowners. In Herefordshire a colony of Normans followed a Norman cousin of Edward's, who became the Earl of Hereford and built the first Norman castle in England.

So, there were two different influences at work in Edward's reign. The Saxon was rougher, tougher and less civilized than the Norman. This difference can be seen also in the sort of churches built by the two peoples (*pics. 2 and 6*).

The country and the people

In 1042 England covered roughly the same area as it does today. But there were marked differences between the separate parts of England. The North (Northumberland and Durham) looked more to Scotland than to London for

2 Harold enters the Saxon church at Bosham in this scene from the Bayeux Tapestry. Compare this building with the more elegant Norman buildings in *pics. 6* and *61*.

3 The King in council with his Court of Ministers, the *Witan*. The Court met regularly during the year at different places — Winchester, Salisbury, Westminster and so on.

fellowship and leadership. South of the River Tees as far as Watling Street was the old Danelaw — the area which had been occupied since the ninth century by the Danes. The area was Danish in character and custom, although less so further south, around the Humber, the Wash and the Trent valley. In the far South-West lived the Celts. These people had been first conquered by the Romans and then driven west from Southern England in the later invasions by the Anglo-Saxons. The Celts — or South Walians as they were sometimes called — were racially different from the people living in Kent, which was the richest of the non-Danish areas, and the lowlands of the South.

The total population of England was only about one and a half million and most of these people lived on the coastal strip between the Humber and the Thames. There were few towns of any size; only London had more than 10,000 people. York, Lincoln and Norwich (*pic. 42*) had fewer than 1000 houses each, with populations of about 6-7000. Oxford, Thetford and Ipswich, with about 800 houses each, had populations of about 5000. Other towns had populations of about 1000 each. The majority of people lived in small villages, earning their living from farming.

The greater part of the country was covered in forests and marshes, wild moorland and wasteland from which some people won a primitive living.

The feudal system in Edward's time

A "feudal" system of society had developed in the ninth and tenth centuries, partly because there was no adequate means of communication between the King and the people living away from London and the people needed someone to look to as a leader and protector. The King's Court of Ministers, the *Witan* (*pic. 3*) met at different places during the year, to try to keep in touch with the affairs of the whole kingdom. But the King's control of his kingdom was really very limited.

Under the feudal system many parts of England had been put under the rule of one of the King's most important followers, called *thegns*. In return for the rights the King had given him over the land, the thegn had to fight in the King's army in time of war, and maybe maintain a village church, for example.

In Edward's time the thegn was owner of all the land in his area. He kept some of it for himself, and the rest he rented out to other farmers, who paid him for the land, not in money, but in kind — by giving him some of the food they produced on it. Or they might pay by working for a spell of time on the thegn's estate. Some of them had to work for two, and some for three days a week. At busy times of the year, such as haymaking (*pic. 38*) or harvesting (*pic. 40*) they had to do extra work, or "boon work".

4 A primitive plough. This one was pulled by only two oxen. Sometimes the soil was so heavy that farmers had to use six or maybe eight oxen to pull the clumsy wooden plough.

Some of the inhabitants of a thegn's area, called *geneats*, had more land and a higher status. They paid the thegn for their land in a different way: they had to provide the thegn with armed escort when he travelled, do guard duty at his home or provide him with horses.

The farming system

The basic unit of the feudal system was the village. This was usually part of the thegn's estate, built near his manor house. Around his house would be his own private park. The village would normally consist of a few houses, a church, a common and an ale house.

The land attached to the village was divided into two or three huge open fields (*pic. 35*). Each of these huge fields was divided into strips and each farmer would have a certain number of strips in each of the fields. This ensured that no one had all the good land while someone else had all the poor land.

5 The great open South Field at Laxton, Nottinghamshire. Large fields are divided into strips, as in medieval times.

In the three-field system, only two out of the three fields were ploughed each year, with primitive ploughs (*pic. 4*). One field was left fallow each year and given a chance to recover from its two years' use. Animals were allowed to graze in this field and their manure would help to improve the quality of the soil.

Each village was surrounded by a large common, sometimes of about 5000 acres. Here the villagers were allowed to graze their animals, collect berries and nuts, firewood and wood needed for building sheds and fences.

This medieval system of farming still continues, as you can see from *pic. 5* of the open fields at Laxton in Nottinghamshire.

The feudal system and the farming system will be further described later on in this book, since they were developed under William the Conqueror. They have been described at this point as a reminder that the system was not introduced to England by William and the Normans, as is often said. Indeed, in many ways England's feudal system was more advanced than Normandy's in 1066.

6 This piece of the Bayeux Tapestry shows the body (*corpus*) of Edward the Confessor being taken to his funeral in Westminster Abbey. Compare this fine Norman building with the rougher church built by the Anglo-Saxons at Bosham (*pic. 2*). Edward had had the Westminster church built in the style of the Normans, which he had come to know and respect when he lived in Normandy.

7 This section of the Bayeux Tapestry shows Harold at his coronation. Notice the Anglo-Saxon Archbishop, Stigand, who carried out the ceremony.

8 In this scene of the Bayeux Tapestry you can see Harold (left) with his hands on sacred objects. He is taking an oath saying that he would support William of Normandy in his claim to the throne of England. The Latin words tell how he took the oath and returned to England.

Edward's death, 1066

Edward died in January 1066 (*pic. 6*) and almost immediately after his burial, Harold Godwinson was crowned King. The coronation took place in Westminster Abbey (*pic. 7*).

However, by becoming King, Harold Godwinson was breaking an oath he had made to William, Duke of Normandy. In 1064 Harold Godwinson had been shipwrecked on the coast of Normandy. At Duke William's court he had then taken an oath (*pic. 8*), promising to support William in his attempt to become King of England when Edward died.

When Harold himself became King, he argued that he had been forced to take the oath at the Norman court in 1064 and that such an oath could not be binding upon a man. He was the son of Godwin and brother to Edward's Queen and he thought that a Saxon ought to be the King of England, not a Norman. The majority of Englishmen agreed with him. His accession was approved by the Witan (*pic. 3*). But, as you would expect, William, Duke of Normandy, was not pleased.

THE YOUNG HISTORIAN

1 Make up a short play on the meeting between William and Harold in 1064 (*pic. 8*).

2 Write the headlines which might have appeared above newspaper reports of (i) Edward's marriage to Godwin's daughter, (ii) Edward's death (*pic. 6*), (iii) Harold's coronation (*pic. 7*), (iv) Harold's shipwreck in 1064.

3 Write the letter which might have been sent by a ploughman (*pic. 4*) after he had visited Edward's Court. (*Pics. 1, 3, 6* and *7* might help. He might have written about clothes, buildings, nobles, their use of Norman French, the new Abbey being built near the Palace and so on.)

4 Make a list of the disadvantages of the open field system (time wasted, animals wandering, disease spreading, one third of the land unused and so on) and then say why this system was used for many centuries.

5 Write the letter which might have been sent by a Norman after he had visited Edward's England. (He might have written about the differences between England and Normandy — the buildings, the landowning, about Godwin and his son, Edward's piety and the new Abbey, Edward's liking for Normandy and so on.)

6 Write the obituary notice which might have appeared after Edward's death.

7 As part of a class frieze, draw or paint any one of the following: (i) Edward on his throne (*pic. 1*), (ii) Harold with Duke William (*pic. 8*), (iii) the new Westminster Abbey (*pic. 6*) and the coronation of Harold (*pic. 7*).

8 Examine *pic. 3*. Explain why these men were unable to govern the country like a modern government does. How does this help to explain the development of the feudal system?

2 The Battle of Hastings and the Conquest of England

Harold and the Vikings

At Easter in 1066 Halley's Comet was seen in the sky. People said that it was a sign that God was angry with Harold, the new King, for having broken his oath to William of Normandy that he would help him become King of England at Edward's death. The Bayeux Tapestry, which was designed and made by Normans, shows the people of London looking up at the fiery comet streaking across the sky and a frightened Harold in his palace (*pic. 9*).

But Harold had more than comets to worry about. The King of Norway, Harold Hardrada, declared that he had more claims to the English throne than Harold Godwinson, the son of a Saxon thegn — even if he had been named by Edward as his heir and proclaimed King by the Witan (*pic. 3*). Hardrada was going to try to take the crown of England from Harold, and he sailed from Norway, with 300 Viking longships. (The ships of William's fleet, shown in *pic. 10,* were also of this sort.)

Harold's army and Stamford Bridge

Harold gathered his army together to march north to fight the Norwegian invaders. One part of his army was made up of the thegns (see page 9) and men they brought with them from the villages. A second part of the army came from the small towns whose people paid for a certain number of well-

9 The Bayeux Tapestry was designed and made by Normans. In this section they have depicted (left) some Londoners looking in at Harold's coronation. (You can see this group in *pic.* 7 too.) In the centre are other Londoners pointing to the comet (*stella*) which was taken to be a sign that God was angry with Harold for letting himself be crowned King and forgetting his oath that he would help William come to the throne. Harold is shown on the right.

13

armed men to fight for the King on their behalf. A third part consisted of the King's own bodyguard or *huscarls*. These were paid soldiers who would be rewarded with land when their service was finished.

This army marched north and met the Norwegians where they had encamped at Stamford Bridge. At the Battle of Stamford Bridge in September 1066 many hundreds of Vikings were killed, so that only twenty-four of their 300 ships sailed back to Norway. It was a great victory for Harold of England.

William's army

However, even while he was rejoicing in this success, Harold was told that Duke William had sailed from Normandy to claim the throne of England which Harold had once promised him (*pic. 8*).

▲
10   Another section of the Bayeux Tapestry shows part of the fleet in which William brought his army from Normandy. The ships are Viking longships — the same kind as were used by Harold Hardrada and the Norwegian invaders. In three of the ships you can see the holes through which the oars were pushed to drive the boat along when there was no following wind to fill the large sail. Notice the large paddles which acted as rudders, the shields, the horses, and the figure-heads on the fronts of the ships.

◀ 11   The knight struggles to get into his armour — his shirt made of chain-mail. It was obviously very difficult to get it on. Notice on the left the chain-mail leggings on another man and the heavy sword at the knight's feet. In *pic. 56* you can see a knight's servants carrying his armour and weapons.

12   William's men build the castle (*castellum*) at Hastings in this scene from the Bayeux Tapestry. Notice the primitive tools used to dig the ditch and throw up the earthen mound or motte in the centre. Most of this work was done by captured Saxons who were treated almost as slaves.

▼

14

The Normans were descended from Vikings and sailed across the Channel in Viking longships (*pic. 10*). William's followers to England numbered about 6000. They were mostly from Normandy, although there were a small number from Flanders and Brittany. They did not come because they owed William duty or service. (Harold's army, on the other hand, did consist of men whose duty it was to fight for him.) William's followers came because they hoped that, if he won, William would reward them with gifts of land in prosperous England.

Norman armour

The Norman knight, dressed in his chain-mail (*pics. 11* and *56*), was well protected. He carried a heavy sword and a protective shield (*pic. 13*) as he rode on his war-horse. This must have been a very strong animal to have carried such a heavy weight.

The Battle of Hastings

William's army landed at Pevensey Bay on 28 September 1066 and then made their base at Hastings, because it was easier to defend. Here they threw up a wooden and earth castle, into which they could retreat if the English should manage to defeat them in battle (*pic. 12*).

Harold and his men came quickly back from Stamford Bridge. They were exhausted when they got back to the South. Harold decided to put his army on a ridge near Hastings. From here, he thought, he would be able to attack the Normans if they advanced, while they would find it hard to charge up the hill at his army.

13   The death of King Harold, as shown in the Bayeux Tapestry. Notice that he and his followers wore the same sort of armour as the Normans (*pics. 11* and *56*). In the bottom of the tapestry you can see servants helping a knight to get dressed.

On 14 October 1066 the Normans moved out from their camp to meet the English army. There were between 6000 and 7000 men on each side. A priest who was with William's army wrote about the Battle. Three times the Normans attacked but, wrote the priest:

> the Saxons hurled back spears and javelins and weapons of all kinds. You would have thought to see our men overwhelmed by this weight of weapons. The English had the advantage of the slope and profited by remaining within their position. Then our foot-soldiers and the knights from Brittany panicked and broke in flight before the English, and the whole army of the Duke was in danger of retreat for they believed that their Duke was killed. But William took off his helmet and, standing before them bare-headed, he cried "Look at me well. I am alive and by the Grace of God I shall yet prove victor." Then the Normans pretended to retreat. The barbarians gave rapid pursuit but the Normans, suddenly wheeling their horses, surrounded them and cut down their pursuers so that no one was left alive. Twice was this ruse employed and then they attacked those that remained alive. At last the English began to weary while the Normans threw and struck and pierced . . .

By nightfall Harold had been killed and the English army was absolutely defeated.

William to London

After the battle, with his rear guarded, William made his way to London to get himself crowned King. He crossed the Thames at Wallingford and approached London from the north through Buckinghamshire and Hertfordshire. He destroyed villages as he went — to show the English that they had better submit to his rule. Various Saxon nobles did so. Saxon Bishops and even towns such as Winchester, the seat of the treasury, also promised to support him.

The people of London at first declared bravely that their King would be Edgar Atheling, William's cousin, but a Saxon. However, news of the way in which William treated the villagers of nearby Hertfordshire and of the submissions of so many of the Saxon thegns forced the Londoners to think again.

Within weeks of the Battle of Hastings they sent a message to William to invite him to his coronation at Westminster Abbey.

William was crowned on Christmas Day 1066 while his followers, scared by a false alarm of English treachery, were setting fire to houses in the nearby village. The noise of the fire and the cries of panic brought William and the priests from the Abbey — a reminder to him that he was not really safe on his newly-won throne.

William had sent men ahead of him to London to build a fortress there. This fortress was of timber, but later on it was rebuilt on the same site in stone. In *pic. 14* you can see the Tower of London as it is today. The square building in the centre is the White Tower, and this was the fortress, or fortified palace, put up by William the Conqueror. Maybe he intended it to frighten the people of London. Maybe he wanted a safe place to which he could retreat if ever they rose up against him. For he was, after all, a usurper and a foreigner.

Norman landowners

As King of England, William claimed that all the land in the country belonged to him. He took possession of the estates of the Saxon thegns who had died at Hastings, and drove from their holdings even those who had survived and had sent him messages of support. As owner of all the land, he could share it out as he wished. He kept one quarter for himself (*pic. 16*). The Church, which had previously owned about one quarter, was allowed to keep its land. The rest of the land was divided between William's barons — mostly important Normans who had supported his attack on England. At this first sharing out of the land, about 170 barons were given holdings. These barons then sublet the lands they had received to other barons.

14   The Tower of London today. The White Tower, the fortified palace put up by William the Conqueror, is in the centre.

15   Part of Offa's Dyke, near Chirk — the raised ▶ earthwork dividing England and Wales, built in the eighth century.

Some of the barons became owners of vast stretches of land. Roger of Montgomery, for example, held large portions of Sussex, Surrey and Hampshire, as well as estates in Wiltshire, Middlesex, Hertfordshire and several other counties. His largest estate of all was the seven eighths of Shropshire. This was a fine reward for service.

On the other hand, William was careful that the lands with which he rewarded even such a loyal servant as Roger should be scattered around the country. Roger and the other barons who were given land would be kept busy riding from one of their estates to another, and they would find it difficult to raise an army of their own from the tenants of their scattered holdings. William, himself a rebel and a usurper, was always frightened that one of his followers might take it into his head to try his own luck at driving a King from the throne to set himself up as usurper-king. By dividing their holdings, William weakened the power of his important followers.

Military service

Under the feudal system William now demanded that all the barons to whom he had granted land should provide him with a fixed number of knights for his army. Similarly the barons demanded that the other barons, to whom they had granted part of their lands, should provide them with a certain number of knights. The barons first of all kept their knights (men who could fight on horse-back) as members of their household, but as time went on, the barons began to let part of their land to their knights. The knights thus became holders of estates like the thegns of before the Norman Conquest. In return for the land granted to them, the knights had to do military service for the baron, their overlord.

Wales

In *pic. 15* you can see part of Offa's Dyke as it is today. This raised earthwork stretched along the present border between England and Wales. It was built in the eighth century by a Saxon King, Offa. Behind it the Celts, who had been driven from their English homeland by the Anglo-Saxons, maintained their Celtic language and religion.

William the Conqueror did not invade Wales, but he did place three of his most powerful barons at the strategic towns of Hereford, Shrewsbury and Chester and allowed them to plunder Wales whenever they wanted. In time the Normans conquered Lowland Wales, building castles (Chapter 4) as they went.

William did not mind allowing powerful barons the ownership of vast lands on the border (or "the Marches") of England and Wales. He hoped that they would be kept busy holding back the Celts or extending their own landholding in Wales. This would keep them from having thoughts of using their power against him.

The harrying of the North

The South of England was soon in the hands of the Norman landowners who built their castles as a sign of their power (Chapter 4). In the North most of the land remained in the hands of the Saxon landowners. The Earls Edwin of Mercia and Morcar of Northumberland, who had fought with Harold in the Battle of Hastings, told William that they would submit to his kingship and he decided, at first, to keep them as earls, although they lost their influence in State affairs.

However, in 1068 and 1069 the North rebelled. Earls Edwin and Morcar were important leaders of the general revolt of 1068, but this was quickly put down and the Earls were pardoned by William. In the 1069 rebellion, in which the Earls did not take an active part, the North received help from the Danes. This time William himself marched north with his army to extinguish the rebellion, destroying as he went.

People, cattle, houses, were destroyed in Yorkshire, Cheshire, the Midland shires and in the more northern counties of Durham and Northumberland. Between York and Durham William left no house standing and no human being alive. Seventeen years later, when the Domesday Book was compiled, there were still scores of villages without any inhabitants. There would be no more rebellions from this area. William was now in full possession of all England. Durham Castle and the Cathedral (*pic. 61*) rose as symbols of the new era. The Normans had conquered.

THE YOUNG HISTORIAN

1   Make a short play about Londoners and Harold when they saw the Comet (*pic. 9*).
2   Write the account which might have appeared in English newspapers of the Norman invasion fleet (*pic. 10*).
3   Write the account of the Battle of Hastings as it might have appeared in newspapers printed in (i) Normandy and (ii) England.
4   Explain why William built a castle at Hastings (*pic. 12*) and a Tower in London (*pic. 14*).
5   Write the letter which might have been sent by an Englishman watching the Tower of London being built (*pic. 14*).
6   Make a chart to show how in the feudal system "every man had his lord".
7   Why did William not try to conquer Wales? (See *pic. 15*).
8   As part of your class frieze, paint or draw one of the following: (i) the knight in his armour (*pic. 11*), (ii) the invasion fleet (*pic. 10*), (iii) the Battle of Hastings (*pic. 13*).
9   Explain why William terrorized the North of England but not the South.

19

3 A New and Stronger Monarchy

The King's estates

Edward the Confessor had had more power over his country than any King of any other country in Europe. The King of France, for example, had little control over nobles — such as William, the Duke of Normandy — who really were the rulers of their regions.

Having come to the English throne, William wanted to make himself as powerful a King of England as Edward had been. His Norman barons, on the other hand, wanted to become as powerful in England as the nobles were in France. As William tried to increase the power of the Crown, he therefore had to try also to lessen the power of the barons.

When he divided up England William kept one quarter of the land for himself. He was easily the most important landowner and would have more money and more feudal followers than any other baron. In *pic. 16* you can see where William and his Norman successors had royal forests and royal homes.

Palaces

In addition to the royal houses and castles, William needed large halls where he could meet his barons in council, just as Edward had. There was one royal palace at Gloucester, another at Winchester and a third at Westminster where Edward had once reigned (*pic. 1*). William also had his White Tower (*pic. 14*) where he stayed.

The King's travels

William travelled to meet with his barons at Gloucester at Christmastime, at Winchester at Easter and in London at Whitsuntide. All his barons had to attend. The King wore his crown and surrounded himself with his advisers to show his barons how important he was.

William spent a good deal of the year travelling between his castles, so that he could hunt in one of the royal forests and collect the food rents and other payments due from the tenants of his land. The rents paid were then used to feed his advisers and the people in the Court (*pic. 17*).

A journey from one castle to another — on poor roads, through many dark forests, with slow horses and clumsy carts — was a major operation. And when the King travelled, all sorts of things had to go with him: wine in casks (*pic. 56*), and the King's treasure — gold plates and cutlery and so on — as well as official documents which he might want to consult.

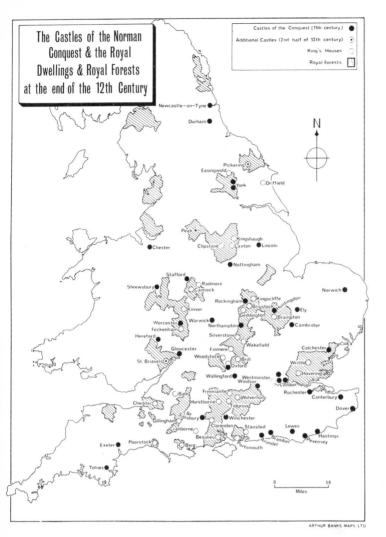

The Castles of the Norman
Conquest & the Royal
Dwellings & Royal Forests
at the end of the 12th Century

Castles of the Conquest (11th century) ●
Additional Castles (2nd half of 12th century) ◉
King's Houses ○
Royal Forests ▨

N

ARTHUR BANKS MAPS LTD

17 On the left of this section of the
Bayeux Tapestry you can see King
William and his guests at table. Notice
the almost complete absence of cutlery
on even the King's table. On the right
William is shown with his half-brothers,
Odo, Bishop of Bayeux (left) and
Robert, Count of Mortain (right). It
was Bishop Odo who commissioned
the tapestry to be made, commemor-
ating William's conquest of England.

▼

Travels and the barons

On his many journeys round the country the King could keep an eye on his barons. He did not trust them, As we saw on page 18, he made sure that he gave no very large areas to any one man — except along the Marches of Wales and also the border of Scotland. The rest had fairly small, scattered holdings in different parts of the country. Each noble was thus surrounded by many neighbours, who would watch for any sign that he was building up his forces to use against the King. It would be impossible for any noble to gather an army of supporters without the King's learning about it as he travelled around.

The King's officials

Unlike today's sovereign, King William and the following Norman Kings of England really did have to govern the country. There was no Parliament, and so it was the King who made the final decisions about matters. The King did have his own chosen advisers in Court, however. Many of these were churchmen — archbishops, bishops, priests or abbots.

Since the King was all-powerful, the people who had the greatest influence over him were those who came into daily contact with him in his household. Among the most important of the King's officials were the various chamberlains of his Bedchamber. (The word comes from the French word for "bedroom" — "chambre".) The King's treasure was kept in his bedchamber and the chamberlain who looked after the treasure became known as the Treasurer. The Master Chamberlain had entire charge of the Chamber and was one of the highest officials. The King had his writing done by a chaplain or priest who sat behind a screen ("Cancella" in Latin). He became known as the Chancellor. The Norman Kings issued many documents and laws, and so his job became more important as the Norman period went on.

There were numbers of less important servants in the King's household. We read of the washerwomen, the tailor, the baker, the tent-carrier, the blacksmiths, grooms, cooks, slaughterers and the many other menial servants who were needed to make sure that the King lived well.

Domesday Book (pic. 18)

William was determined to make sure that the King remained in control of the whole country. He needed to know therefore exactly what his country was like and who his tenants were. In 1086 the King's advisers sent out messengers to make a survey of every part of England. They gathered together the people of every village and asked them many questions. Who used to own the land in the time of King Edward? Who owned it now? How much land was used for ploughing? How many teams of oxen were used? How many pigs, cattle, sheep and horses were there in the village? How many acres were covered in woodland? How much in commonland? Every baron and knight had to give an account of their lands: how much they owned, farmed, rented out; how much

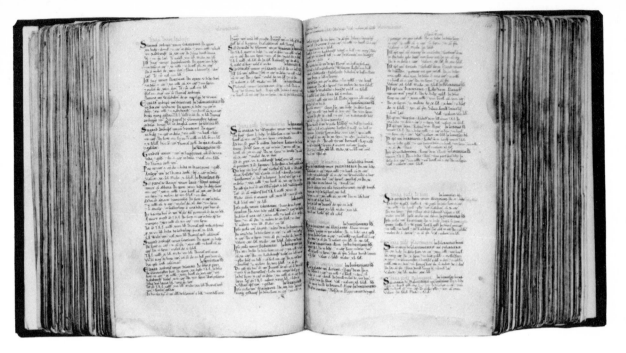

18 Domesday Book.

they received in rent from tenants; how many tenants they had . . . and so on.

The results of these enquiries were written out by hundreds of clerks in the hundreds of villages throughout the country. The whole lot was collected together in the one huge report known as *Domesday Book*. The book was called "Domesday" book because people in the twelfth century compared the great enquiry made by the King's messengers with the Last Day of Judgement. The book is now kept in the Public Records Office and students can see it if they want to *(pic. 18)*. It was written in Latin, but fortunately for us, this has now been translated. If you go to your local library they will tell you where you can see the Domesday description of your county.

After the book had been compiled William knew everything there was to be known about his kingdom. He knew exactly what taxes ought to be paid by each baron and knight and by each village. His advisers were able to send messages to his local officials — or shire-reeves (sheriffs) — to tell them what taxes they had to collect for the King in their district. These taxes poured into the King's treasury.

This is one example of how the King built up the power of the central government, his government. He now had a picture of the whole kingdom.

The Oath at Salisbury
Every man who owned land as a tenant had to take an oath of loyalty to his immediate overlord — the man who had granted him the land. So, the knight took an oath of loyalty to the baron, and the baron took an oath of loyalty

23

to the more important baron from whom he had received his land (see page 17). "Everyman had his lord" is a way of describing the feudal system.

Now, William wondered, what would happen if a baron rebelled against the King? Would the baron's feudal followers, who had taken their oath of loyalty to him, support him or the King? To make sure that they would support the King rather than their immediate overlord, William called together all his barons and their more important feudal subjects in 1086 and made them all take a solemn oath that they would serve the King first before keeping their oath to serve their feudal overlord. The oath taken to the King was called the Oath at Salisbury because it took place on the wide grassy plains near that town.

We have to remember that an oath (*pic. 19*) for men in Norman times was an extremely serious, religious agreement between a man, his earthly lord and God. Since men in Norman times took their religion seriously, they were extremely unlikely to break an oath. The Oath at Salisbury made it almost certain that no baron would rebel against the King, because the baron would know that he would get no support from the men who had now promised loyalty first of all to the King.

Edward Freeman, a great historian, believes that when the Oath at Salisbury was taken, "England became forever a kingdom, one and indivisible . . . ".

William's Norman successors

King William died in 1087. He was succeeded by his son, William II, known as William Rufus because of his red hair (*"Rufus"* is Latin for "red-haired".) He was a cruel and unpopular King who allowed his barons too much freedom. Few people mourned him when he died in 1100. He was killed by an arrow while

◀ 19   Taking an oath. The two men here with their hands on sacred objects (the Bible and the cross) are the plaintiff and the defendant taking an oath before the judge.

20   Henry I crossing the English Channel. ▶ Notice the rudder paddle, the holes for the oars, the fixed sail and the figure-head.

hunting in the New Forest in Hampshire. Some people think that he was shot deliberately.

He was succeeded by his brother Henry I (*pic. 20*), a very active and wise King. He travelled as his father had done to make sure that the power of the Crown was maintained. He increased its power by setting up a new system of travelling judges. These King's Judges travelled throughout the country, to try the more important cases. This took some power away from the barons who tried cases at their own baronial courts on their estates. It also helped to build up a system of national law: the King's Judges met each other when they returned to the King's Court, and in their discussions of the cases they had heard and the decisions they had given, they agreed on a system of law and a scale of punishments. Their presence throughout the country showed that the King's power was growing as the barons' power grew less.

Stephen and Matilda

Unfortunately, Henry I's son was drowned at sea. After the death of Henry I on 1 December 1135 there was a long period during which his daughter, Matilda, tried to claim the throne, while a baron, Stephen, a grandson of King William argued that no woman had the right to rule. Stephen declared himself King in December 1135 "by the Grace of God, with the consent of the clergy

and the people, elected King of England, consecrated by William, Archbishop of Canterbury and confirmed by Pope Innocent".

The Civil War between the followers of Stephen and those of Matilda went on for nineteen years. The barons used this period to build up their own power while the power of the Crown was weakening. They raised armies from their estates to fight for one or other of the royal claimants. They changed sides during the struggle, taking bribes from both sides and winning permission from both Stephen and Matilda to build more castles. They used their power to plunder the countryside and enrich themselves at the people's expense.

The Plantagenets

Matilda's husband was the Count of Anjou (*pic. 21*). Their son, Henry, married Eleanor of Aquitaine. In November 1153 Matilda and Stephen signed a Treaty at Wallingford by which she recognized Stephen as King of England while he

21 Matilda's wedding feast on her marriage to Emperor Henry V. There are knives on the table but no other cutlery. Notice the servants, who are drawn much smaller than the noble characters

adopted her son, Henry as his heir. Stephen died in 1154 and Henry became King of England as well as Count of Anjou, Tourraine and Maine and Duke of Aquitaine.

Henry was the first of a new line of Kings. He was not a Norman. His father, a French nobleman, was Geoffrey Plantagenet, so Henry II was the first of the Plantagenet Kings of England. However, we ought to note that during his reign, 1154-1189, Henry II did his best to follow the policies of the Norman Kings, William I and Henry I. He made the barons pull down the castles they had built during the Civil War. He sent out trained men to run the government of the counties. He set up a jury system to replace the barbaric method of trial by ordeal and in so doing made the Crown more powerful than it had been under William I or Henry I. In this he was, in one sense, a Norman.

THE YOUNG HISTORIAN

1 Look at *pic. 16*. Show how the King's power increased under William the Conqueror.
2 Why did the barons resent the increase in the King's power? How did they try to limit that power during the reign of King Stephen?
3 Why did the Norman Kings spend so much of their time travelling around their kingdoms? (See *pic. 16*.)
4 Write the letter which might have been sent by one of the servants who travelled with the King from castle to castle. (You might get some help from *pics. 16, 17, 35* and *56*. He might have written about the officials, horses, furniture, the roads, slowness of the journey, the work he had to do once they got to the next castle.)
5 Why did the King and his advisers want a survey of the kingdom as contained in Domesday Book? (See *pic. 18*.) Why was there little to report about the districts of Yorkshire and the North? (See page 19).
6 Write the letter which might have been written by a villager after he had been questioned by the messengers compiling Domesday Book. (He might have mentioned the questions, other villagers, the local baron and the questioning, the power of the new King, and so on.)
7 Write the newspaper headlines which might have appeared above reports on (i) the division of land by William the Conqueror, (ii) the King's arrival at one of his great palaces, (iii) the decision to make a survey of the whole country and (iv) the taking of the Oath at Salisbury.
8 Make a short play about each of the following: (i) a baron changing sides during the Civil War, (ii) the taking of the Oath at Salisbury.
9 As part of the class frieze, paint or draw (i) the King in Council (*pic. 17*), (ii) a journey by the King's party, (iii) the King at table (*pic. 17*) and (iv) the taking of the Oath (*pic. 19*).

4 The Barons and their Castles

Why so many castles?

The Normans defeated the English army at Hastings in 1066, but English opposition continued for some years. The harrying of the North was needed to subdue that region (see page 19), while Hereward the Wake's resistance in the Fenland was not put down until 1071.

The Normans knew that they were hated and in danger of attack, and so the first buildings they put up were defensive castles. William's invasion fleet (*pic. 10*) included ships carrying sections of prefabricated timber castles which could be put up quickly to provide the Normans with immediate protection. They were built in a hurry and could easily be set on fire. In time the Normans learned to build in stone. But the castles which, at first, sprung up over the whole of England were as primitive as the one which William put up as soon as he had landed (*pic. 12*).

22 A prisoner in the Tower of London

▲
23   Castle Rising, Norfolk. You can see the bridge over the moat, leading from the inner bailey to the outer bailey where there would have been buildings for the baron's servants and animals. Only the keep still stands — it must have been the best-protected part of the castle.

24   Pembroke Castle. The round keep was the place to which the lord would go for safety if the enemy got past the walls and gates. On the right you can see the main gateway, protected by its own system of towers and battlements. Notice, too, that opposite the main gateway was another major structure where the baron had his living quarters.

▼

29

Where were the castles built?

If you look at *pic. 16* you can see the sites of some of the major Norman castles in England. The Tower (*pics. 14* and *22*) was built before William moved into London for his coronation. Like the first castle at Hastings, the first Tower of London was a wooden building.

In London, Lincoln, York, Cambridge and elsewhere the Norman barons chose the best sites for castles — overlooking the neighbouring town from a hill or hillock, which made them more difficult to attack.

Building a castle

A great earthen mound was first made by digging a huge circular ditch and throwing up the earth into the centre. The mound, called a motte, was sometimes 100 feet in diameter. The motte and ditch had to be built quickly — this work took only five days in London, eight in Dover and eight for a second castle in York in 1069. Many Englishmen must have been recruited into slave-gangs to enable the huge work to be done so quickly.

On top of the motte a wooden tower (keep) was erected, and the motte and ditch were enclosed by a wooden stockade. Below, as further protection for the keep, a sort of outer court — called a bailey — was surrounded by another stockade and often, also, by another ditch. A castle like this could withstand the sort of attack which might be mounted by enemies in the eleventh century.

Later castles

Once they had more time, the Norman barons employed stone-masons to build larger, stronger and better-protected castles out of stone. In *pic. 23* you can see one such castle. The lord's keep on the motte was surrounded by a moat — the ditch which was sometimes filled with water. The area inside the moat was called the inner bailey. Crossing the bridge over the moat, you came to the outer bailey and buildings for the baron's servants and animals. This was protected by another moat. In the event of an attack the bailey would be sacrificed first while the lord would withdraw to the stronger and better-protected motte.

Wales

The conquest of Lowland Wales took place during the twelfth century. One symbol of that conquest were the stone fortresses, such as the one at Pembroke (*pic. 24*). The fortress was built on a hill and surrounded by a moat. Its massively thick walls could resist almost any attack. If the enemy got past the walls and gates, however, the lord could escape to his round keep.

Life in the castle

The Norman castle was built to resist attack and not as a place of comfort.

The most important room in the castle was the great hall. This was an all-purpose room: trestle-tables put up for mealtimes (*pics. 17* and *27*) were taken away at night-time when the hall was used as a bedroom. The privileged few might be able to use the benches as beds. The rest slept on the floor. The stone slabs of the floor were normally covered with rushes. These were rarely changed — except when the King was expected.

▲
25 The curtained beds of a very rich nobleman or a monarch. Few people enjoyed such luxury in Norman England.

26 Castle Hedingham, Essex. You ▶ can see the narrow slits through which air got into the various rooms. These were called "wind's eyes", from which we get the modern word "windows".

The richer baron in a larger castle might have one or two rooms set aside as bedrooms. He might have a personal bed (*pic. 25*), but most people slept in the hall in their normal clothes, covered only by a heavy cloak.

The hall was a draughty place since there was no glass in the slits in the walls (*pic. 26*). It was also smoke-filled, for there was no chimney to take away the smoke from the great log fire which burned in the centre of the hall.

Eating in the castle

The main meal was eaten between 10.00 a.m. and 11.00 a.m., while a light supper was served between 4.00 p.m. and 6.00 p.m. For the main meal the baron and his followers could have several dishes. There was beef and pork, mutton, poultry and eggs. In winter most of the meat eaten was salted. Fresh meat was not available in the winter because there was not the food to keep many animals alive throughout the winter months. Since hunting was one of the main amusements of the landowners (*pics. 28* and *87),* their tables were often graced by the venison, partridge and other game birds that they or their guests had caught.

The baron and his guests did not have all the accessories we would expect to find on a modern table. There was a table cloth, but there were few, if any, dishes. Diners sometimes shared one dish between two. Meat was served, often from a spit carried to the table by a servant, straight on to a four-inch-thick slice of bread. There were few knives and no forks so that fingers were used to pick up meat, vegetables, puddings and cakes. Eating was a messy operation, and hands were washed before and after the meal.

Wine, mead or ale to drink was passed in a cup from hand to hand for people to take a mouthful as they wished. Only the very rich had their own cups; the majority had to share — and risk the danger of catching some disease or other.

When the diners rose from the table, the servants merely tipped the remaining food — bones, jellies, fruit — on to the floor where it was attacked by the dogs or rotted in the rushes.

27   At this medieval royal banquet there is still no cutlery and few dishes even on the table of the King at Court. Notice the servants kneeling.

28 Hawking in October, taken from a medieval manuscript.

The young squire

If you look at *pics. 17* and *27* you will see the servants kneeling. They might be the sons of the household or sons of other noblemen sent to the home of their father's noble friend to be trained as knights.

Boys of noble families were sent away from home to live in a baron's castle when they were seven years old. They served as a personal servant, or page, to the baron. The baron taught the boy how a member of the upper class had to behave, to ride a horse and fight on horse-back and to use a sword and lance. When he was fifteen, the boy became a squire and followed his lord in battle, on hunting expeditions and into tournaments (*pic. 83*). The squire carried his lord's shield and weapons, helped to dress him in his armour (*pic. 11*) and looked after his horse. Only when he was twenty-one was he considered ready to become a knight. At the knighting ceremony, the baron, or sometimes the King, would take the young man before the other knights in the castle or at a tournament or battlefield, and tap him on the shoulders with a sword, present him with his spurs and tell everyone that from now on the young man was to be called "Sir —— ".

Hawking and hunting

The favourite sport of the Norman barons was hunting. Some forests were kept for only the King to hunt in. Others were kept for the local baron. Some were open to anyone. Hunting gave the baron and his guests exercise, training in riding which made them an efficient cavalry in wartime, and the chance to add to the supply of food for the castle table.

Hawking, or falconry, was an ancient skill of Egypt and the Middle East. It had come to Europe around the fifth century when the Roman Empire was about to collapse. The British learned it around the ninth century. The Normans were great falconers and treated falconry both as a sport and as a means of getting extra food.

As in most other things in Norman England, there was a class system in falconry. Men of different social ranks were allowed to hunt with a particular kind of falcon only. The King's bird was the jerfalcon; an earl was allowed a peregrine falcon; a yeoman (freeholding farmer) could use a goshawk; and a priest a sparrow-hawk.

Much time and patience was spent training hawks to catch and bring back their prey. Larger hawks caught big birds — pheasants, heron and geese, while smaller hawks caught such birds as larks.

Barons, castles and later Norman kings

A baron could build a castle only if the King agreed and gave him the licence to do so. The King could thus make sure that none of his barons had too many castles or grew too powerful. During the reign of the inefficient William Rufus (page 24) and during the Civil War (page 26) barons took the opportunity to build many unlicensed castles in which to build up their power. During their reigns Henry I (page 25) and Henry II (page 27) ordered the destruction of these unlicensed castles. One of the major features of the Norman period was the continual see-sawing struggle between Kings, anxious to build their power, and barons, seeking to maintain or even increase their power.

THE YOUNG HISTORIAN

1 Explain why the Normans built so many castles. Do you think that they were right to be frightened of the English? Why?
2 Give a newspaper account of the building of a wooden castle (*pic. 12*).
3 Look at *pics. 12, 23, 24* and *26*. Write a short article on "The changing pattern of castle building".
4 Give an account of an attack on a castle as it might have been written by (i) the attackers, and (ii) the defenders. (They might have written about the walls, gates, weapons, hill, moat, food and drink.)
5 Write the letter which might have been sent by a guest at a castle. (He might have mentioned the hall, furniture (*pics. 17, 25* and *27*), eating (*pics. 17* and *27*), etc.)
6 Give an account of a day spent hunting or hawking (*pic. 28*).
7 As part of a class frieze, draw or paint one of the following: (i) mealtimes (*pics. 17* and *27*), (ii) the hall, (iii) hawking (*pic. 28*), (iv) building a castle (*pics. 12, 23, 24* and *26*).
8 Make up a short play on the building of a castle. You might think of the conflict between the baron and the owners of houses that had to be pulled down to provide the room for the new building; the work of the gangs of Saxons needed to dig the ditch and make the mound; the Norman craftsmen needed to build the walls, whether of wood or stone.
9 Make a poster advertising "The Knighting of Squire Fitzurse".

5 The Knights and their Manors

The grant of the manor and land

We have seen that William the Conqueror kept about one quarter of all England as crown land (page 20). He also gave large grants of land to the Church (Chapters 10 and 11). The rest was split into about 6000 districts which were

29 The manor of Boarstall in Buckinghamshire. The manor house is the large building on the right of the church. The village has grown near the manor house. At the bottom is a picture of a man paying homage to his overlord, the knight. You can see the fields divided into strips and the surrounding commonland with trees and animals.

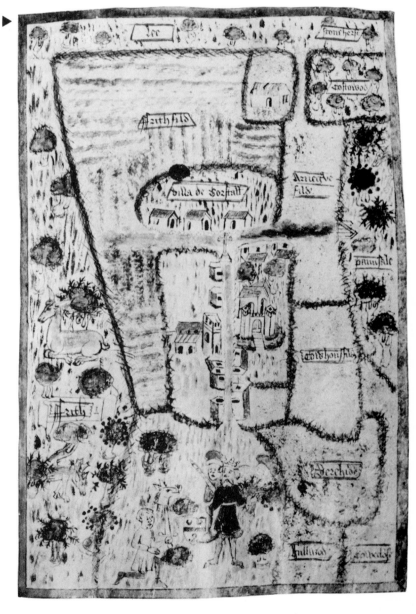

30 In the background is a plough pulled by horses — a sign that the soil was light. The harrow in the foreground was a tool which broke up the soil after it had been ploughed. This made the ground better for the seeds, which were planted, as you can see, by throwing them by hand. (See also *pic. 4*.)

shared amongst the barons. Eventually, as we saw (page 18), the barons granted land to their knights, who then became lords of their districts, similar to the thegns of Saxon times.

The knight normally built a large house of stone on his land in which to live and kept part of the land as his own private estate, surrounded by a stone wall. A village, with its church and ale house, grew up outside the wall. Attached to the village were the open fields of farmland and the common. In *pic. 29* you can see how one knight, Roger, kept part of the land granted to him for his own private use, and how the village grew up around his estate. The knight's house was called the manor house. The entire village community was known as the manor, and the knight was lord of the manor.

The manor house — a nerve centre

The manor house was more than a living-house: it was also the centre of the economic life of the manor.

Farming was the main occupation of the people in the village. They ploughed, sowed, reaped and mowed according to the seasons and under the watchful eye of the reeve (*pic. 31*). Their ploughs were primitive (*pics. 4, 30* and *36*) and the work hard. We shall study the work of the farmers in Chapter 6. Here we ought to note that the manorial farmland was divided into three huge fields (*pic. 5*) which were divided into strips. Each villager was allotted a number of strips in each field, and paid rent for them to the lord of the manor either in money or, more usually, in kind. One tenant would bring eggs, another some honey and a third some meat, varying in value according to the amount of land allotted to them. Surrounding the fields were the manorial wastes or commonlands where, as we have seen (page 11), the villagers grazed their animals, collected berries and nuts in the forests and gathered wood for fires and for building.

The knight in the manor house did not run his estate on his own. He had a steward to help him and maybe clerks if he owned several manors. If a knight had several manors he would have a bailiff living in each one who would handle the daily work of the manor. There would always be a reeve who decided when the tenants had to work on the lord's strips and fields and who had to do what job during harvest time or during haymaking (*pic. 31*). The bailiff or steward laid down how much rent was due from each villager and was responsible for the collection of the rents.

The manor court

The lord of the manor sat as head of the manor court to hear disputes between villagers — someone accused of theft, or of fighting, or of damaging another villager's property. The manorial lord was judge and jury in such a court. When the number of King's Courts (page 25) grew throughout the country, the power of the manorial lord started to decline.

31 A reeve supervises the work of peasants. Notice their clothing and the sickles. The straw was cut only halfway up the stalk. What remained would be ploughed back in as manure.

32 The barn at Godmersham — once the great hall of the manor.

The hall (*pic. 32*)

The most important room in the Norman manor house, as in the Norman castle, was the great hall, which acted as a dining-room, court-room, sitting-room, community centre, public house and bedroom. In smaller manor houses everyone lived together. In the larger ones extra rooms were built on to provide some privacy for the master and his wife — so that they could sleep in their own rooms away from the soldiers and servants. In time they might even have their own sitting-rooms where the women could sew in peace away from the noise and dirt of the hall.

Life in the manor

Life in the Norman manor house was far from luxurious. There was very little furniture. As in the castle, trestle-tables were put up in the hall at mealtimes and taken down again to make room for other activities. The floor might often be only the beaten earth, although normally it was covered in stone slabs. Rushes were strewn to make it less cold — and when they were fresh the hall smelt sweetly. After a short time the stale food, animal droppings and other litter on the floor made the place stink. Lack of washing facilities meant that clothes and bodies too were rarely washed (*pic. 33*). This added to the smell. The manor hall was not a very healthy place.

33 Bathing a child in an iron pot which might also have been used for cooking. Only the rich could afford such pots in Norman times.

Self-sufficiency

Each manor was more or less self-sufficient: the village community produced almost everything they needed on their own land. Wool was spun and woven during the long winter evenings (*pic. 54*). Hemp was used to make canvas which served as covering for the window spaces as well as for mill-sails and sacks. Spoons, plates and bowls were carved from beechwood; drinking mugs from wood or horn. (Only the richer manor houses had a supply of gold or silver dishes.) Leather sandals were made at home while the village tanner would make leggings and gaiters. Each village had its blacksmith, who made and

38

repaired simple tools, and its own miller, ale-house keeper and brewer.

Some things did have to be bought in — salt (for preserving food), iron, dyes, for example. Pedlars carrying such goods in their sacks travelled from village to village. Visitors who were also welcome at the manor were minstrels and other travelling entertainers (Chapter 13).

Life was very simple. The year was controlled partly by the demands of agriculture (Chapter 6) and partly by the festivals of the Church (Chapter 13). No work was allowed on the major festivals of the Church — of which there were about one hundred in the year, while there was always a week or so of celebrations connected with the three great festivals of Christmas, Easter and Whitsun.

The people's food

The lord in his manor and the people in their simpler homes ate much the same food, which was produced locally. During the spring and summer they ate much fresh meat — beef, pork, lamb and mutton. This diet was varied whenever a chicken was killed, a rabbit caught or when a partridge or pheasant fell victim to some bird of prey (page 33). During the autumn most of the

34 A medieval angler fishes in the stream near the castle.

animals in the village were slaughtered because there would be no food to keep them alive through the winter. The meat of the slaughtered animals was salted to preserve it and throughout the long winter the people had only this salted meat to eat. They used spices to make it taste different.

Fish was an important part of the weekly diet. The Church forbade the eating of meat on Fridays, and on other days during the six weeks of Lent, before Easter. Many villages had a neighbouring stream as a source of fish (*pic. 34*). Others had fishponds where fish were bred.

Very few vegetables were grown. The potato was not known in England until the seventeenth century. Cabbages and others of our common vegetables were also unknown in Norman times. Peas and beans were grown, and fruit was cropped from orchards and trees growing wild in the woodlands on the common or wasteland. But there was a general lack of foods containing Vitamin C, so that scurvy was a common disease, as was leprosy.

Two fields were sown with grain. A bad harvest would mean there was no flour — and thus lead to starvation. It is not surprising that there was a high death rate among the people of Norman England. Many children died in infancy, many others died before reaching the age of ten, and few people lived beyond the age of thirty. Norman England was an under-developed country, its people making a poor living out of their main occupation — farming (Chapter 6).

THE YOUNG HISTORIAN

1   Look at *pic. 30*. Explain why this ploughman produced less per day than the modern farmer. How does this help to explain his lower standard of living? What does this tell you about the value to us of technological development?

2   Look at *pic. 32* and imagine the hall being used (as in *pics. 17* and *27*). Write the letter which might have been sent by a guest at the hall. (He might have written about the tables, floor, ceiling, fire, food, smells, servants and so on.)

3   Write the letter which the lady of the manor might have sent after the delivery of the first bed (*pic. 25*).

4   As part of the class frieze, paint or draw one of the following: (i) the three fields of the village (*pic. 29*), (ii) a plough (*pics. 4* and *30*) and (iii) the hall (*pic. 32*).

5   Make up a short play involving the reeve (*pic. 31*) giving orders to the tenant farmers.

6   Look at *pic. 34*. Why was fish a more important part of the diet of the Normans than it is of the modern Englishman? Can you suggest why the stream was important — other than as a source of fish?

6 Farming

The different classes of landholders

In 1066 in the South and the East there was a well-established manorial system, under which different classes of people had different rights and different amounts of land.

After 1066 the lord of the manor might be either the baron or the knight to whom he had given land. Below the lord of the manor came the freemen, the villeins, the cottars, and, rarely, the slaves. The freemen, or socmen, owned the thirty strips of land – the virgate – which were allotted to them. They were free to sell their land and they were asked to perform only some of the extra, boon work, needed on the lord's land at busy times of the year, such as harvesting.

▲

35 The open fields at Braunton, Devon. The fields are still divided into strips.

◀ 36 The primitive plough which needed two men to work the oxen and the plough.

The majority of the villagers were the villeins. A villein also had thirty strips of land — ten in each of the fields — but he had to pay rent in kind for this — giving some of the produce of his land to the lord. He had to do regular weekly work on the lord's estate, under the supervision of the reeve — and not just the boon work at busy times. Sometimes a lord might reward a villein for some special service by making him a freeman.

Below the villeins were the cottars who were allotted only about five strips. And below these were the slaves, or serfs, who had no land of their own. They worked for the manorial lord and for the other villagers who paid them by giving them food. Each strip of land was often an acre in size. To make sure that nobody had an unfair share of good or bad land, the strips allotted to each villager were scattered in different parts of the three open fields (*pic. 35*). One of the three fields was left fallow each year, to allow the soil to improve.

The North

The Midlands and the North — the Danelaw — were areas which had once been ruled by the Danes. Here the freemen owned their own compact farms and there was no manorial system. The Normans had to struggle to extend the feudal system to these regions with their tradition of independence.

The year's work on the farm

Whether in the South or the North, however, the work of the people was regulated by the weather and the seasons of the year. We can make a calendar as an aid to our study of medieval farming:

January

The only outdoor work that could be done was ploughing (*pic. 36*). Indoors the oats were threshed (*pic. 41*) to provide seed for spring sowing.

February

Ploughing continued while some crops were sown. The reeve and the bailiff directed the villagers in the sowing of barley, oats, peas, beans and vetch for animal fodder. Some men and teams of oxen were set to harrowing the ploughed land. The harrow (*pic. 30*) was a frame with spikes set in it. It broke up the soil into smaller pieces and so helped germination. Other teams of men were put to collecting branches that had fallen during the winter storms and gathering leaf mould and animal manure to spread on the fields.

37 After ploughing and before harrowing (*pic. 30*) heavier soil had to be broken up by people using large wooden sledge-hammers. This was dirty, hard work.

March

This was the month for pruning fruit trees, planting herbs and vegetables in the kitchen gardens around the cottages and looking after the vineyards. Wine was produced in large quantities in the manors in the South of England, mainly on monastic lands. It was never of high quality because there was not enough sunshine.

April

The field which had been left fallow for a year was ploughed for the first time. There would be more ploughing before it was sown with wheat to be harvested in September.

May

This month the animals which had been kept alive during the winter were allowed out to pasture on the fresh grass. Under the supervision of the hayward, some men built fences to stop the cattle getting in to the growing oats. Now that the soil had had a chance to dry out, teams of men and women were sent out with wooden sledge-hammers (*pic. 37*) to break up the clods of earth on the newly ploughed fields, while others were put to digging ditches around the fields to help drainage.

June

Haymaking began (*pic. 38*). Everyone had to help during this month — including the freemen who did their boon work. Hay waggons needed repairing with timber gathered from the forest or the common or taken from the lord's own forest. The haymaking was supervised by the hayward who had to make sure that nothing was stolen or eaten by animals. The hay would be precious food for the few animals kept alive during the winter.

July

During the last weeks of June and the month of July the sheep had to be washed and shorn (*pic. 39*). After the shearing the animals were fattened for sale to the butchers in the nearest market town. July was also the month for weeding the cornfields, getting rid of the thistles and giving the fallow land its second ploughing to destroy the weeds that had grown up during the fine weather.

August

In this harvest month every man in the manor had to give a hand again, to reap, bind and store the corn. The corn was cut halfway up the stalk with sickles (*pics. 31 and 40*). The remaining straw was either collected to be used for thatching or ploughed back into the ground as manure. When the harvest was safely stored in the barns ready for the winter threshing, people went to gather timber for fences and winter firewood. They also gathered fresh rushes for floor covering (page 38) and brushwood if they needed to repair the roofs of their houses.

September and October

The fruit was picked, honey was collected from the hives and the villagers made cider from the apples, perry from the pears and ale from the barley. As they did not use hops, the ale quickly became sour.

November

Animal manure was taken from the yards and spread over the fields. Then, before the winter frost, the fallow land was given its third ploughing and sown with a winter crop of rye or wheat. The wheat and barley — but not oats, which were threshed in January — were threshed (*pic. 41*). If the harvest had been a good one, there would be plenty to eat for the lord's household, for the villagers and for distribution among the poor, as well as seed for the next sowing. But if the harvest had been bad, the villagers had to go hungry

▲

38 Haymaking was a pleasant task since it was done in the summer. The hay would be used as winter fodder for the few animals kept alive during the winter.

39 Shearing a sheep. The wool would be prepared by women and children (*pic. 54*) to make cloth.

▼

44

throughout the long, damp winter. During November the pigs were driven to the woods to feed on acorns and beechnuts. The other animals were examined to see which ones should be kept alive during the winter. The rest were either sold or kept for slaughtering until late December — since they could forage for nuts, which made enough food to keep them alive, until then.

The mill

During the last two months of the year the corn had to be ground to produce the flour for making bread. Each manor had its mill, normally owned by the lord who charged his tenants for having their corn ground. The miller, who also made a charge, was often accused of taking more than his fair share of flour and was often a very unpopular man in the village. Some villagers ground their own corn using grinding stones or pestles made of wood or stone, but this was forbidden by the lords of most manors. Their officials used to make checks to make sure that the villagers were not depriving their master of his income from milling in this way.

Improving and enlarging the manor

The Normans took the manorial system in to the North and the Midlands. They also increased the size of the manorial holdings wherever they could.

The Norman landowners made their estates more efficient than they had been under the Saxons. They had to, because the King imposed high taxes on his barons, the knights and the tenants, and so that they could pay these, they had to make their land produce more.

40 A close-up of the process of harvesting grain — in this case barley. See *pic. 31*

41 Men use a flail to thresh oats. The flail was a hinged stick. As you can see, the grain was knocked out of the oats. It was collected when the reeve (*pic. 31*) thought that there was no more grain left in the ears of oats.

One sign of the greater efficiency was the growth in the number of men who became specialists in one aspect of farming. There had always been the miller. Now there came the shepherd, swineherd, hayward and cowman — all of whom had only one job to do on the estate. They became expert at their tasks and so improved the quality of farming done on the estate. This led to increased production so that more food was available for sale in the towns. Indeed, the towns could not have grown as they did, had it not been for the high quality of Norman farms. We shall study the growth of towns in Chapter 7.

THE YOUNG HISTORIAN

1   Write the letter which might have been sent by a ploughman (*pic. 36*) about breaking up a new field. (He might have written about the need for the new field, what they hoped to grow on it, the need for three ploughings, clod-breaking (*pic. 37*), and harrowing. He would also have written about the weather, the team of oxen and the hard, slow work he had to perform.)

2   Why did people have to break up clods of earth (*pic. 37*)? What does this tell you about (i) the efficiencies of the ploughs, and (ii) the nature of the soil?

3   Write the letter which might have been sent by someone during the hay-making season (*pic. 38*). (As guide words you might take some of the following: length of the day; the pleasant nature of the work, compared with ploughing; the involvement of the whole village; the importance of the hay for the animals in the winter.)

4   Write the newspaper reports which might have appeared after (i) a good harvest, and (ii) a bad harvest. Why was there always a danger that England might suffer from famine?

5   Examine *pics. 36, 37, 40* and *41*. What evidence is there that Norman farmers produced much less in a day's work than does the modern farmer? What effect did this low productivity have on the people's standard of living?

6   The Normans had no printed books. They had to rely on monks to produce handwritten and highly decorated scripts. Make a calendar in this style in which your decorations show the work done on the farm in the different months.

7   As part of the class frieze, paint or draw (i) shearing (*pic. 39*), and (ii) threshing (*pic. 41*).

8   Make up short plays on (i) a Norman knight introducing the manorial system into the old Danelaw, and (ii) a knight giving a villein the privilege of being a freeman.

7 Towns and Townspeople

Towns in Domesday Book 1086

Between 43 AD and 410 AD the Romans had built a number of fine towns throughout England. Many of them were fortresses, or *castra*, from which we get the suffix "chester" as in Manchester. But the Anglo-Saxon invaders had destroyed most of these towns and built none of their own. By 850 AD most of the Roman towns were in ruins. When the Vikings invaded England they set up fortified settlements, or *burhs*, from which we get the word "borough". The Saxons under King Alfred built similar strong points. Traders and crafts-men settled within earthen walls for protection.

One of the attractions of England for Duke William of Normandy was its wealth, a good part of which came from a flourishing trade. This trade — in wool, cheese, corn and other products — was centred on the towns which had grown strong again as the Danes and the Saxons had learned to live together.

In Domesday Book we can read about all these towns. Chester had 282 houses, Lincoln 730 — a reminder that Norman England was primarily an agricultural country, with a small population of which only a minority lived inside the walls of towns (*pics. 42* and *43*).

Why did towns grow?

Before 1066 every borough was the King's. Only the King could give permission for a town to be built; and he received the tolls collected at the town gates from merchants who came to sell their goods in the market. All the existing boroughs remained as King's boroughs in Norman times.

However, from 1066 many feudal lords encouraged the growth of new towns on their own estates — so that they could take tolls from their boroughs just as the King did from his. Feudal lords who wanted to start a town or borough on their land had first to get the King's permission for a market or fair to be held. Once they had that permission, some lords, who had enough money, actually built their own town. They laid out streets and building plots and built churches, and rented out plots inside the town walls to people wishing to live there. The townspeople were called burgesses (from the old word "burg" for town). Otherwise a town grew up around the market, without any action by the lord, because of its site. For example, a town would grow where there was a monastery because of the employment available in a monastery (Chapter 11). And towns also grew up around castles, such as the one in Pembroke (*pic. 24*), because of the demands for goods from the people living

42   This plan of Norwich is dated 1573 — therefore after Norman times. But it
shows how the town was surrounded by walls and how the gates were set in the walls
at convenient points. People in small towns like this were never far from the countryside and fresh air.

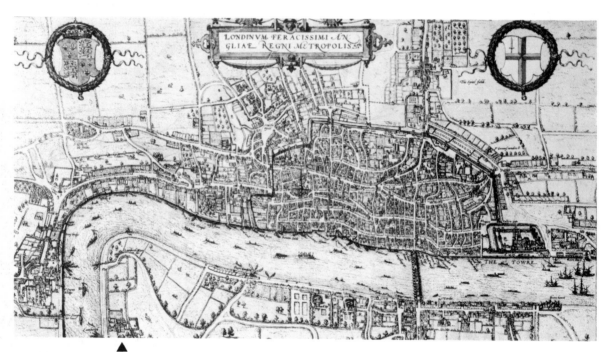

43   Plan of London, the leading port.

in the castle. Other towns grew up at crossroads or at river crossings. Ox*ford*,
for example, grew up where the Thames was easily forded. The growth of
trade led to the building of new ports. London (*pic. 43*) remained the leading
port, but Bristol grew as a centre for trade with Norway and for the wine trade
with France. King's Lynn grew as more wool was exported from the Fenland.

Towns were free

Men came to live in towns because these were the centres of trade. Inside the town's walls men felt more protected. Above all, they welcomed the chance to be free of any feudal overlord. The burgess in the town looked down on the villein in the manor — the unfree peasant who lived in his primitive hut and worked at the command of a reeve of bailiff.

The townspeople were possessive about their freedom and suspicious of all outsiders who came to the town. Outsiders were "foreigners". None of them were allowed to stay in the town overnight. When outsiders came to the town with goods to sell at the fair or market they had to pay a toll as they came in and left the town and they were subject to the laws passed by the leading burgesses or town council.

Walls and gates

In *pics. 42* and *43* you can see that Norwich and London were each surrounded by a wall. This gave the townspeople a sense of protection. Gates were set into the walls and were opened at first light to let in the people coming to the market; the gates were locked at night, by which time all foreigners had to have left the town. The remains of medieval walls can be seen at Chester, York and other towns, while the sites of town gates have been commemorated in the names of streets in many modern cities and towns.

The town and its traders

The greater part of the population of every town were the merchants, the craftsmen who also sold the goods which they made from their shops, their apprentices and unskilled workers.

The merchants formed guilds or societies, each organizing the people involved in one particular trade. In *pic. 44* you can see the sign of the Company of Grocers. There were guilds for fishmongers, wine sellers, and so on. The leading members of the guilds played a large part in the government of the town.

The craftsmen were also organized in guilds — for goldsmiths, saddlers, silversmiths, carpenters and so on. The members of a craft guild paid a weekly subscription to the officers who ran their guild. In return they would receive a welfare payment whenever they needed it — in times of sickness or when they were too old to work — and the guild would also look after the widows of deceased members.

The guild officers had to make sure that the members of the guild upheld the honour and dignity of their craft. They examined the workshops, inspected the goods being made and sold, and laid down the hours during which craftsmen were allowed to work and the number of apprentices they could take on.

A boy became an apprentice to a master craftsman who taught him the "mysteries" of the craft. When he had learned enough as an unpaid apprentice — usually after seven years — the guild officers allowed him to become

49

a "journeyman" who was employed by the day — paid a wage for each day's work. The word "journeyman" came from the French word for day: "*la journée*". After some years a journeyman could ask to be recognized as a master

44 The coat of arms of the Company of Grocers, a merchant guild. The guild would regulate the trade of grocers — see that the weight and quality of the goods they sold were correct, and prevent outside grocers coming in and underselling the guild members.

45 A guild officer examines the work of an apprentice mason and the carpenter who wishes to become a master carpenter

46 A fish merchant makes a sale to a lady. It is not clear whether the boy is a merchant's assistant or a servant of the lady.

craftsman. In *pic. 45* you can see a guild officer examining the work of an apprentice mason and a carpenter. The latter is preparing his "masterpiece" which, if good enough, will qualify him to become a master carpenter.

The streets of the town

People coming in from the villages found the streets of the towns noisy and exciting places. There was a continual stream of traffic: waggons and pack-horses carrying goods to and from the market, and from the workshops of the various craftsmen *(pic. 57);* and animals being taken to market or to the slaughterers. And there was a constant shouting of people advertizing their wares. Sellers of fish *(pic. 46)*, meat, pies, cakes, clothes, shoes, cutlery and other goods had to rely on their voices to attract passers-by.

The members of each trade tended to have their shops and workshops all together in one area. Some evidence of this exists in the names of streets: Poultry in London was where the sellers of chickens met; Butchers Row in Salisbury was the meat market, while Baker Street was where one went to get bread and cakes. This grouping together of members of one trade made it easier for the members of the guild to keep an eye on each other and for the guild officers to keep an eye on all their members.

Disease

The narrow streets of the towns were the source of a great deal of disease. The main streets might be cobbled but the side streets were nothing better than mud tracks, beaten down by the hooves of animals and the wheels of the waggons. There were no pavements, and no systems of drainage or of refuse collection. People threw rubbish from their homes, dyers emptied their vats, and other craftsmen swept the litter from their shops out on to the street. Animals roamed the streets, scavenging among the decaying vegetables, old bones, scraps from the pastrycook's and other shops. Over all was the smell of decomposing matter.

Few of the towns had a proper water supply. London had a number of open channels bringing water from springs to public fountains. But in London and in most other towns people relied on wells and streams for their small supply of polluted water, often "thycke with vapours and infect with frogges and other worms" *(pic. 47)*.

It is not surprising that plagues and epidemics were frequent and that the death rate was very high. One thing that saved the towns from being any more dangerous was that they were so small — and therefore no one lived so far away from open ground and the countryside which lay outside the town walls that they could not get some healthy air.

The government of the town

The burgesses of a town elected aldermen who in turn elected one of their

47   People collecting water in jugs
from the well. Unclean water was a
source of disease.

number as the mayor. The aldermen and mayor formed the town council.
It had to try to keep rubbish off the streets, and to maintain the town's prison,
roads, bridges, walls and gates. The council was also involved in the building of
the market, the town hall and other public buildings. The council collected
tolls from people bringing goods or animals into the town and from foreigners
taking goods out, and the money thus raised was used to pay for the work
ordered by the council. However, the council had no part in the provision of
housing (Chapter 8) or of churches, of which there were a large number in
every town, as we shall see in Chapter 10.

THE YOUNG HISTORIAN

1 Make three columns each containing the names of six towns whose names end in (i) -burgh or -borough or -bury, (ii) -ford, and (iii) -chester or -eter.

2 Some towns grew around monasteries, others around castles or around abbeys. Find six examples of each.

3 Write the newspaper article which might have been written to explain the growth of a town around a monastery. (What was produced on the monastic lands? What things did the monastery have to buy? Why did many people visit monasteries? How would this have called for the growth of shops, inns — and a town?)

4 Write the letter which might have been sent by (i) an abbot asking for permission to hold a fair or market on his land, and (ii) the King agreeing to this request.

5 Imagine that you were a villein who had come into a town for the first time. Write the account which you might have given when you went back to the manor. (What would you have noticed? Walls? Gates? Noise? Dirt? Shouting? Craftsmen in their workshops? Animals? Food for sale? Houses? Churches? Various kinds of officers and their clothing?)

6 Look at *pics. 46* and *47*. How do they help to explain the high death rates in towns in Norman England?

7 Look at *pic. 44*. Make or draw a coat of arms for some other trade — wine sellers (Vintners), fishmongers, etc.

8 Make a poster advertizing "Market Day".

9 Make up a short play on one of the following: (i) becoming a master craftsman, (ii) officers punishing a dishonest craftsman, (iii) a Norman street, and (iv) a council discussing the rebuilding of the town wall.

8 Home Life

Lack of comfort

We have seen how the King at a royal banquet (*pics. 17* and *27*), the Norman baron in his castle (Chapter 4) and the Norman knight in his manor house (Chapter 5) had few of the things that are considered necessary for comfortable living today. They had no dishes, no beds, no glass in their windows. The majority of people, who lived in the small villages must have had even less comfortable homes. They worked long hours in the fields (*pics. 30, 31, 36*, and *37*) to reach a poor standard of living.

The ordinary home

Most peasants lived in a cruck house. You can see the shape of a cruck house in *pic. 48*. The cruck was a curved timber which supported the roof. It was made from an oak branch split into two identical halves which were set into the ground and joined at the top. A cruck was put up at each end of the house-to-

be and the two crucks were joined across the top with a ridge pole. The crucks were also joined lower down by other beams, called collar-beams. This strengthened the framework, lessened the thrust of the roof and made it possible to put in side walls. Upright posts were set in the ground on each side and joined to the lower collar-beams, to form the framework of the side walls.

48   The interior of a farm house in Conway, North Wales. You can see the cruck and the collar-beams which formed the framework for the roof.

49   Harold at table upstairs in his home at Bosham. Only well-off people could afford to have upstairs rooms. This is another scene from the Bayeux Tapestry.

50   A man warms himself by an open fire on a slab in the middle of the floor. He is sitting on a stool. There would have been few such luxuries in a peasant's home. The peasant would have sat on the floor or on a home-made bench.

The walls of the house were made by filling in the framework of the sides and the ends with lighter timbers and with wattle and daub. This gave a pattern of upright posts woven with flexible branches or withies, which was then plastered on both sides with a kind of mud concrete — mud mixed with hair, straw or manure.

In some cruck houses the builders arranged a second row of upright posts inside the first to support another of the collar-beams of the roof. This gave a large rectangular space in the centre of the house which could be used for the family's living quarters, while the space between the two sets of posts was then used to house animals, or as sleeping quarters for the family.

The cruck house was an improvement on the simple hovels in which large numbers of the poorer people lived. For these, two branches lashed together at the top were used for each end of the house. A ridge pole joining the two ends also supported all the sloping side timbers which were set in the ground or in a low wall of mud. The roof was made by covering the timbers with turfs cut from the earth, the grass facing inwards, or with a thatch of rushes.

The majority of better-off peasants were happy in their cruck house with its earthen floor. Bedding consisted of straw, rushes or furze spread on the floor. In the winter this gave little protection from the cold of the frozen earth, or from the damp when the thaw set in. The warmth provided by the animals living under the same roof as the humans was more welcome than the smell.

Upstairs

In *pic. 49* you can see that some people built homes with an upstairs loft large enough to be used as storage space or as sleeping quarters. Only the very well-off would have been able to afford the bigger timbers, stronger poles and floor planking required for such an arrangement. A simpler way to enlarge the cruck house was to add further pairs of crucks and ridge poles to make a long house. The family then lived at one end and the animals at the other.

Warming the home

We have seen that the great hall of the castle and the hall of the manor house (*pic. 32*) had no chimneys. It is not surprising then that the peasants' homes had no fireplaces or chimneys either. The usual way of warming the home — castle, manor or cruck house — was to have an open fire. This was sometimes held in an iron basket in the middle of the room, but only the wealthy could afford such a luxury. In the cruck house the fire was made on a slab in the middle of the floor (*pic. 50*). There was no chimney to take away the smoke, and so the air in the house was even more contaminated than it would have been with just animal breath and the stench from manure mixed with straw in the stabling area and from the rotting food in the rushes on the floor.

51 Cooking for a rich household (another part of the Bayeux Tapestry. The section shown in *pic. 17* follows to the right of this). The servants on the left are cooking the food over an open fire, well away from the main building. It was then carried by other servants to be tasted before being sent in to the King and his guests.

52 Feeding the chickens was one of the jobs done by the ▶ women.

53 The home of a prosperous merchant — the Jew's House in Lincoln.
▼

Cooking and eating

The main food eaten by the ordinary people was a coarse black bread made of flour from barley, rye, bran or a mixture of wheat and rye. Breakfast of bread and home-brewed ale was eaten at about 6.00 a.m. At 10.00 a.m. the men came in from the fields to have their dinner of bread, butter, cheese or eggs. Sometimes there was meat — fresh in the summer and salted in the winter. At about 4.00 p.m. they came home again to have supper. For this they ate bacon, bread or oatcake, a gruel or stew, with ale to drink. The stew would be cooked in an iron pot set over the open fire (*pics. 33, 51* and *54*). In the homes of the rich, meat would be roasted on a spit and prepared by cooks in a kitchen set some way from the house (*pic. 51*). In the ordinary home the cooking was done on the open fire in the living quarters — which added to the dirt and smell in the home.

Women's work

While the men went about the heavy work in the fields the women were left at home to look after the children and the animals. They milked the cows and ewes, made cheese, brewed ale and made clothes. Every villager had a small plot of land attached to his house. Here the wife would tend a garden of vegetables, herbs and other plants. She also fed the chickens (*pic. 52*) which provided the family with eggs, and meat when a chicken was killed.

Also, of course, the women would prepare the great pot of gruel for the evening meal (*pic. 54*), taking care to keep the fire going, and adding vegetables and — when they had it — meat to the pot.

Town houses

So far we have looked at the houses and lives of the people in the village. But a minority of ordinary people lived in the small, walled towns. Here the richer merchants or craftsmen had a two-storeyed house. On the ground floor was the shop or workshop, opening on to the street. Behind this were the hall, main room and living quarters of the family. Upstairs was a family living-room. Some homes had only two rooms — one up and one down. The upstairs room then had to serve as bedroom and living-room for the whole family.

If you look at *pic. 53* you can see the Jew's House in the Steep Hill, Lincoln, a narrow medieval street. Although the house has been much altered since it was first built around 1150, enough of it remains to show that originally it had a centre doorway which opened into a passage from front to back. There was also a first-floor room with two windows and a wall chimney which you can see over the central doorway. This was the home of a prosperous merchant. The less well-off craftsmen would have had a smaller house than this, while the unskilled worker would have lived in a hovel which looked more like the primitive village hut than this grand town house.

Clothing

The manor was almost entirely self-sufficient. The villagers did most things for themselves, including making clothes. They spun the wool from their own sheep (*pic. 54*), wove it into cloth and made the simple garments which were worn by the majority of the villagers. These were a hood, a tunic, cross-gartered trousers and, for the fortunate, leather boots. If you look at *pics. 30, 31, 36, 37, 38, 39* and *41* you will get some idea of this clothing.

Richer people wore better clothing. The baron and knight wore a kind of underpants. To these were attached pieces of linen, wool or soft leather, which made a sort of stocking to keep the legs warm. They wore soft leather shoes, sometimes coloured and with pointed toes stuffed with wool. These were lighter and more comfortable than the heavy boots worn by the peasant.

The lady of the castle or manor also wore an undergarment beneath her gown. The gown was pulled in with a belt around her waist. Some gowns were made with bodices laced to fit closely. As time went on, people learned to cut and make clothes to fit the individual, with seams at the back and front as well as under the arms, but this did not happen until the end of the period we are studying. It was achieved by the skilled workers who formed their own Guild of Tailors. There was also a guild for shoemakers, who were known as Cordwainers because the best leather came from the Spanish town of Cordova. Craftsmen like these, however, supplied clothes only for the richest people in the country — the baron and his lady, the knight and his womenfolk and, perhaps, the families of the more prosperous merchants.

54 Preparing wool on a spinning wheel while someone else gets on with cooking the gruel in the big pot over the open fire.

THE YOUNG HISTORIAN

1 Imagine that you are an Englishman of the eleventh century who has travelled from Norman England on a Time Machine to live in your present home. Write an account about (i) dining in Norman England and in modern England as you have found it, and (ii) furniture in Norman England and in modern England.

2 Why was the cruck house (*pic. 48*) an improvement on the hovel? How did some people make it even more comfortable?

3 Look at *pics. 48, 50* and *54*. What features of Norman life would you have found most objectionable? Why?

4 Divide a sheet of paper down the middle. On one side make illustrations to show the sort of food eaten by the Norman workers and their families. On the other side show the sort of food eaten in ordinary homes today. You might use cut-outs from magazines to decorate this piece of work.

5 What evidence is there that the Norman diet was less well-balanced than ours? Why was this a cause of ill-health? Can you think of other reasons why the Normans were less healthy than we are?

6 Look at *pic. 53*. Why was life even in this rich home noisy, dirty and cramped?

7 Look at *pic. 44*. Now make a coat of arms for either the Tailors or the Cordwainers, adding a short note to explain what you have drawn or painted.

8 As part of the class frieze, paint or draw (i) the cruck house (*pic. 48*), (ii) cooking (*pics. 51* and *54*), (iii) women at work (*pics. 52* and *54*).

9 Make up a short play on "Building the cruck house".

9 Trade-Inland and Overseas

Country and town

The Anglo-Saxon pattern of trade was not changed when the Normans came to England but the volume of trade both inside the country and between England and countries overseas increased after 1066.

Country people were more or less self-sufficient, although as we shall see, even they had to buy some goods. The villagers took their surplus produce — eggs, milk, cheese, as well as animals — to the town where it was bought by the townsfolk. In the towns no one was entirely self-sufficient and people could make their living by this. The better-off landowners and the richer towns-people also bought goods which were imported into the country by overseas traders — silk, precious gems, spices, wine, oil, brassware, glass and other luxuries.

◀ 55 A picture of men going out in small fishing boats from a stained glass window in Canterbury Cathedral.

56 This piece of the Bayeux Tapestry reveals the poor conditions of travelling. The rich rode on horseback; the poor walked. Goods — iron, wool, fish, as well as wine, shown here in its barrel — had to be carried over the rough roads in bumpy carts, which were sometimes pulled by men.

▼

Fish

Fish was an important part of people's diet in Norman times. The Church forbade the eating of meat on Fridays and on many other days during the year. During the six weeks of Lent leading up to Easter it was normal for people to do without meat for two or maybe three days each week as a penance, or punishment. Fish was eaten instead.

Some villagers managed to catch fish for themselves in the local stream (*pic. 34*), but not every village had a convenient or productive stream. People living in the towns had to rely on men going out in small boats (*pic. 55*) and bringing in fish to sell in the town (*pic. 46*).

Iron

Iron was another product in great demand — for tools (*pics. 31, 36* and *38-41*) and for pots (*pics. 51* and *54*), as well as for weapons (*pics. 11* and *56*). Iron could not be transported far across country from the areas where it was naturally available to those where it was not, and so there were some parts of England where iron was never seen at all. Other parts of the country had their own iron pits. Areas such as the Forest of Dean became famous iron centres, and Gloucester owed its growth to its proximity to these ironworks.

Wine

While the peasants drank home-brewed ale, the Norman barons and knights preferred to drink wine at table. Some of this was produced in England (page 43) but better-quality wine was imported from Spain, France and Germany. In *pic. 56* you can see wine in a barrel being transported on a cart. If the wine was being sent a long distance the cart would be pulled by horses. Notice the poor quality of the road and the iron-rimmed wheels which must have rattled over the cobbled streets in the towns and cut deep ruts in the muddy tracks linking one town to another.

Money

In the manor people exchanged goods on a bartering basis, paying the blacksmith with a few eggs, for example. The tenants paid their rents in kind, handing over as payment for their land part of the produce of their strips in

62

the fields. These people had little if any need for money.

But when men bought goods from overseas or bought and sold goods from different parts of the country they had to use money. Norman Kings granted licences to moneyers to mint money in various towns. In 1066 there were seventy mints in the country. Each moneyer got the dies he needed to stamp out the coins from London. The coins normally showed the image and superscription of the King on one side and on the other a cross with the name of the moneyer and the mint.

In small towns there might be only one moneyer, but York had ten and London, the largest town, had twenty. It was easy for these moneyers to cheat — by lowering the quantity of silver in each coin. Norman Kings passed severe laws under which those caught producing "bad" money had their hands cut off and nailed to the door of the moneyer's forge or smithy.

The silver penny was the normal coin. If people wanted to spend less than one penny they used the cross at the back of the coin to split it into half-pennies or farthings (quarters of a penny).

The shop

In *pic. 57* you can see a cobbler's shop and workshop. Although it is an illustration of a Tudor shop, it can be used to get an idea of a shop in Norman England because there was very little change in arrangements between 1200 and 1500. Notice that the shop opened on to the street where passers-by could see the goods on display. Behind the shop was the room where the craftsmen (pages 49-50) worked. Other craftsmen had similar shops with their living quarters on the floor above the workplace.

57   A cobbler's workshop in Tudor times — apart from the people's costume, the shop would have looked very similar in Norman times. Notice the counter across the street. The workshop was behind. You can see the master craftsman (standing, right) supervising the work of journeymen and apprentices.

58   The old market hall at ▶ Chipping Campden in Gloucestershire.

The market

We have seen that before a town was built the King was asked to grant permission for a market to be set up (page 47). Only when that permission had been given would a lord, abbot or bishop go ahead with his scheme for town development.

Therefore, in every borough there was a market place. In *pic. 58* you can see a market hall. Here the various traders set up their stalls, or simply stood or sat around showing their produce on trays or in baskets.

Every day, except Sunday, the streets leading to the market spot would be full of noise. The unsprung carts (*pic. 56*) with their iron-rimmed wheels and the heavy boots of the peasants bumped and clumped and clattered over the uneven cobbles. From the open shops came the sounds of the smiths, carpenters and other craftsmen at work, while traders shouted out to draw attention to their goods.

The noise was aggravated by the narrowness of the streets which were crowded from the opening of the town gates at dawn, until dusk, when the bell tolled as a signal that it was time for "foreigners" to leave the town and for the gates to be closed. The burgesses then went to their homes and a great quiet descended on the unlit streets — which were, however, still clogged with rubbish from the day's trading.

Paying the tolls

When the King gave permission for a market to be set up, this privilege had to be paid for. And so everyone coming to trade in the market was made to pay a toll. In *pic. 59* you can see an officer collecting a toll from a villager who has brought in dairy produce to sell. Notice that these people are merely sitting or standing at the side of the street; they do not have a stall. But they still had to pay for the privilege of being allowed to sell in the market.

People who had stalls paid more. These would be the traders who had more expensive items for sale — clothing, furniture, cutlery and so on. The townspeople who set up stalls paid a smaller toll than the "foreigners" who came into the town for market day. They were also allowed to set up their stalls before the "foreigners" had set up theirs.

London

When towns were first set up there was plenty of room for the few hundred or so houses, churches and other buildings. As the population grew, pressure on the land also grew. Gradually, plots were split up and gardens were built over. London and many other towns grew so much that some of the population spilt outside the walls. Outside the walls of London the population grew around areas such as Clerkenwell, Smithfield, Spitalfields, Moorfields and Southwark. A new stone bridge was built in 1176 to link Southwark and London. In *pic. 60* you can see that people built houses and shops on the bridge — an indication of the shortage of land inside the city itself.

◄ **59** A market scene of fifteenth-century France, which nevertheless shows the collection of tolls as it took place in Norman England. On the right the man with the money bag is taking a toll from the girl who has come to sell her produce in the market. None of these people have stalls from which to sell their goods.

60 A Tudor drawing of London Bridge with its houses and shops. The area at the bottom of the picture is Southwark.
▼

65

Overseas trade

The main reason for the growth of London was its position as the country's chief port, trading with the Continent and other countries. The growth of trade between Europe and the Eastern Mediterranean was a result of the Crusades (Chapter 12). After 1099 there were Crusading kingdoms in Palestine and Syria which themselves had trading links with India and China. Through these new kingdoms Normans and Europeans began to develop trade in new commodities such as silks and spices.

THE YOUNG HISTORIAN

1 Look at *pic. 55*. How do you explain the high demand for fish in Norman England? How does this help to explain the growth of towns along the coasts of England? What other reasons help to explain the growth of these towns?

2 Look at *pic. 56*. Write the letter which might have been sent by someone who had to travel on such a cart. (You might mention quality of roads — dusty in summer, muddy in winter, pot holes, ruts; slow journeys; danger of robbery; getting to a town, its walls, gates and streets.)

3 Write the account which might have been written by a newspaper reporter after a visit to a craftsman's shop and house (*pic. 57*). (He might have mentioned the shop front, the street, the workshop, the master craftsman, his journeymen, apprentices, guild officers (*pic. 45*), and the problem of living above the shop.)

4 Why was it a privilege to be allowed to have a market (*pic. 58*)? How might the town council have used the money collected in tolls (*pic. 59*)?

5 Write the letter which a "foreigner" might have sent to complain of the way he was treated in a town — at the gates, in the streets, by the toll collector, by burgesses, and on leaving the town at nightfall.

6 Look at *pic. 60*. Explain why London grew. Make a plan to show how London was linked with the village at Westminster, with Southwark, and with the fields to the north of the city walls.

7 Write the letter which might have been sent by a sailor after a journey through the Mediterranean to Palestine. (He might have written about the size of the ship, what it was carrying out to sell and what it brought back, how long the journey took, the dangers from wind and sea and from pirates and so on.)

8 As part of the class frieze, draw or paint (i) a fishing boat (*pic. 55*), (ii) a market hall (*pics. 58* and *59*), (iii) the craftsman's shop (*pic. 57*).

10 The Church

The parish church

Look back at *pic. 29*. The village church is the largest building in the village after the manor house. This gives us an idea of the importance of the church and the priest in the life of the Norman village. It was the same in the town. In *pic. 42* there is a plan of Norwich, one of the larger towns of Norman England. In 1086 Norwich had twenty churches and forty-three chapels — a large number of places of worship for a town with fewer than 1000 houses.

The parish priest

In *pic. 2* you can see the style of church building in which the people had worshipped before the Normans came. The old churches continued to be used after 1066, of course, but the Normans built many new churches too (*pic. 61*). In the church the parish priest baptized children (*pic. 66*), married young people and buried the dead. The people came for mass each Sunday as well as on each of the holy days (or holidays) throughout the year.

In some places the priest was a monk from a nearby monastery. (We shall see more about the monastery in Chapter 11.) But in most villages the priest was the son of a local villein or freeman. As a priest grew too old to manage his work in the parish, the people would choose another boy and send him away to be trained as a priest at a school attached to a cathedral or monastery. When he had been prepared for priesthood they asked the bishop to ordain him — that is, to make him a priest.

In some villages the priest was certainly not as educated as the monks in the monasteries, but he had received some schooling and would be the only one in the village who could read and write. This made him even more important in the eyes of the people. He was excused from doing any manual work. The villagers supported him by paying tithes and other contributions.

The bishop

The Church divided the country into dioceses each containing a number of towns and villages (*pic. 68*). Each diocese was looked after by a bishop. Some bishops were in charge of wide areas. The Bishop of Crediton, for example, was responsible for a large part of Devon and Cornwall. Other bishops, for instance the Bishop of Ely, had a smaller diocese.

The bishop had a very large church as his headquarters. This was called a cathedral, from the latin word *"cathedra"*, meaning "seat". Saxon churches

had been small (*pic. 2*), mainly because the Saxons did not know how to construct buildings which required wide roofs. The Normans were better builders, with more technical skill than the Saxons. This can be seen in the cathedrals which they built (*pic. 61*).

The bishop as a nobleman

William had given about one quarter of England's land to the Church. Some of this land was given to monks for building new monasteries, but a good deal went to Norman bishops who had come to support William in his attack on England. Some had merely prayed for his success and others had fought for

61   The nave of Durham Cathedral. Compare this with the Anglo-Saxon church in *pic. 2*.

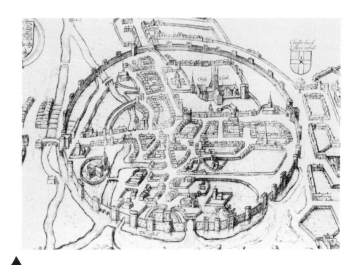

▲

62   A plan of Canterbury showing its walls, gates, neighbouring river and very large cathedral.

63   St Peter with the key depicted in a Norman carving at ▶ Wentworth Church, Cambridgeshire.

him. His half-brother, Odo, was Bishop of Bayeux. In *pic. 17* you can see him beneath his name on part of the tapestry which he ordered to be made and which now hangs in Bayeux. Odo was a soldier-bishop.

Some bishops were as much concerned with their rights as landowners as with their duties as church leaders. Because they were better educated than most other landowners they were the ones whom the King called on to advise him. Along with the abbots (the heads of the monasteries), the bishops were thus the political leaders of the country — and this did not change until the sixteenth century.

Archbishops

A diocese consisted of a number of parishes grouped together. The dioceses were also grouped together to form two big provinces of the Catholic Church in England — York and Canterbury. The Archbishops of York and Canterbury

69

ruled over all the bishops. The Archbishop of Canterbury was, by tradition, accepted as the head of the Church in England.

Bishops and Archbishops had large households of advisers and servants, and these needed supplies of food and a wide variety of other goods. The demands of such households were one reason for the growth of towns (page 47). This is very evident from the growth of Canterbury (*pic. 62*) which became an even more important town after the murder of Archbishop Thomas à Beckett in 1174, for his grave became a place of pilgrimage, visited by thousands of people each year.

The Pope

The Pope was the head of the Catholic Church and was represented in England by a Papal Legate or Ambassador through whom he kept in touch with what was happening.

Before sailing across the Channel in 1066, Duke William had been careful to get the Pope's blessing on his expedition. This was enough to gain him the support of thousands of followers. If we find this hard to understand today, we must remember that in Norman times everyone in Western Europe was a Catholic and believed that the Pope was the representative of God on earth. To remind them of this, many churches contained statues of the first Pope, St. Peter, to whom Jesus Christ had said "to thee I will give the keys of the kingdom of heaven . . .". The people believed that St. Peter, who was represented with the keys (*pic. 63*) and his successor-popes, had a God-given power. It is not surprising that Popes, Archbishops, bishops and priests were very important people in the lives of the people in Norman England.

Church schools

There was a school attached to every cathedral and every monastery. Many of the boys who went to such schools stayed on to become priests or monks. But many of them left school after receiving a certain amount of education. Their training had been "clerical", and so they were known as "clerks" — members of the clerical or clergy group. These educated clerks found jobs in the households of landowners and merchants who welcomed their abilities to read and write.

Church courts

We have seen that William the Conqueror was anxious to increase the power of the Crown. He made a decree that the bishops should no longer take part in trials in the local law courts. But he did, perhaps surprisingly, allow the Church to have its own Courts of Justice in which all members of the clerical class were to be tried if accused of any crime. The Church claimed that this gave it the right to try cases involving not only ordained priests and monks but also the clerks. William, who needed the support of the Church during the first

70

uncertain years of rule, agreed to this. And so two different sets of national courts grew up. There were those run by the King's Judges (page 25) and those run by the Church.

The system of Church and King's courts worked well in William's reign, but in the twelfth century the Plantagenet King, Henry II, tried to limit the powers of the Church courts and his rivalry with the Archbishop of Canterbury, Thomas à Beckett, led to the murder of the latter.

The Church and the Crown

There had also been argument between King Henry I and his Archbishop of Canterbury, Anselm. Anselm denied the King's right to invest bishops with their ring and staff, saying that they ought to receive their power from the Church. The King felt that if he did not invest the bishops with their office, he could not maintain his influence over them. It was necessary that he should have control over the bishops, because they were landowners. In the end it was agreed that the Church should invest the bishops with their ring and staff, but only after they had made their feudal oath to the King.

The people and the Church

Few, if any, of the ordinary people understood the arguments between the King and the Church leaders. They accepted the priest's version of the quarrel, since, after all, he was educated and should be expected to understand what was going on. Furthermore, the people had little time to be bothered with the arguments of the rich and powerful. They were too busy trying to win a poor living from the land. They looked to the Church to provide some glamour to brighten their dull, drab, hard lives. Much of their entertainment was centred around the Church, as we shall see in Chapter 13.

The Church realized that the people had little education and would not be able to follow long, complicated arguments about God, saints, heaven and so on. Religion had to be presented to them in a simple, visual way, and so the churches were built and decorated so that they would act as so many "sermons of stone". The walls were adorned with what we might call visual aids (*pic. 64*). Church furnishings were made by fine craftsmen (*pics. 65* and *66*).

Pilgrimages

Today many people save money throughout the year to go on holiday, while others save for weeks or months so that they can go to a special football match. In Norman times people saved so that they could travel on a pilgrimage to some place connected with a holy man or saint. Some of these places were in Europe, but some were in England. One such place is Bury St. Edmunds. St. Edmund, King of East Anglia, had been murdered by heathen Danes. People thought that his grave was a very special place. They travelled to pray at his tomb and to ask him for some favour. In time a town grew up around

64 This could be called a "visual aid", to explain an idea to people. The devils are shown as women — a warning to men of the danger of sins of impurity. In the bottom picture the woman is a lady of fashion. Jesus is shown in heaven, above.

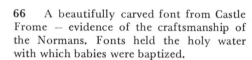

65 A carving of bear-baiting on one of the turn-up seats in Beverley Minster. Obviously men thought of their church as entirely part of their ordinary, daily life — it was not separate — and they decorated their churches with subjects of no religious significance.

66 A beautifully carved font from Castle Frome — evidence of the craftsmanship of the Normans. Fonts held the holy water with which babies were baptized.

the Abbey where he was buried. It was called the "burh" of St. Edmund.

The people who travelled on pilgrimages collected badges to show where they had been (*pic. 67*), and here again we could liken them to some holiday-makers today!

THE YOUNG HISTORIAN

1 Look at *pics. 2* and *61*. Write a short article on differences between Saxon and Norman Churches. Why have Norman churches lasted longer than the Saxon ones?

2 Collect illustrations of Norman cathedrals. You may be able to get photographs or postcards from people who have visited them. Other sources will be illustrated magazines and the advertisements of organizations such as the Post Office, Norwich Union and the British Tourist Board.

3 Look at *pic. 62*. There were a large number of churches in towns such as this (see also *pic. 42*). Can you suggest (i) why people in Norman times built so many churches in small towns, and (ii) why, in proportion to the population, we have fewer churches today?

4 Imagine that you are a Norman parent telling your child the story of St. Peter and the keys (*pic. 63*). Give an account of your conversation with the child.

5 Look at *pic. 64*. Give an account of the sermon which a village priest might have preached using this "visual aid".

6 Write the letter which might have been sent by a pilgrim travelling to or from Bury St. Edmunds.

7 Make a poster to attract support for either (i) the building of a new church in Norman England, or (ii) a pilgrimage.

8 Make up short plays on (i) King Henry I and Anselm arguing about who should invest the bishops, (ii) a priest giving a sermon (*pics. 63* and *64*), and (iii) pilgrims on a journey.

67   A pilgrim's badge of lead. This one shows ▶ the figure of St. Thomas of Canterbury. Badges of other saints were sold to people who visited other centres of pilgrimage.

11 Monks and Monasteries

Anglo-Saxon monasteries

Among the believers in every major religion there are always men and women who want to live apart from the outside world and devote their lives entirely to prayer, reading holy books and serving others in the name of their religion.

68 The boundaries of the dioceses are shown by dotted lines. The names of dioceses are in boxes. The monasteries are marked by the black circles.

69 The remains of the great Cistercian monastery at Rievaulx, Yorkshire. Cistercian monasteries were set in remote places. The Cistercians became skilful farmers.

For example, there are such people today in Shinto monasteries in Japan, Buddhist monasteries in Burma and Catholic monasteries in England.

Before 1066 all the monasteries in England were Benedictine. That is, they followed the rule of St. Benedict. St. Benedict was the abbot of a Catholic monastery near Rome, who in 529 drew up a set of simple rules by which the monks in his monastery had to live. These rules were then adopted by all Catholic monasteries. Later they formed the basis for the rules of new orders of monks.

Benedictine monks had come to England in the sixth century and by 1035 they had a number of monasteries in England (*pic. 68*). There were so many monasteries that few people lived far away from one. Monks and monasteries had a great influence over the lives of the people of an age in which religion was a very important part of man's life.

Other orders

As time went on, not all the Benedictine monks followed the strict rule of their founder. In 910 a group of monks in Cluny in France decided to try to live a stricter life. They became known as Cluniacs. After the Conquest a number of Cluniac monasteries were set up in England — the first being built at Lewes in Sussex. In time, even the Cluniac monks became more concerned with making money and living a comfortable life than with the strict observance of their rules.

In 1098 a group of monks started a new monastery at Cîteaux in France. They wanted to get back to the original strictness of the Benedictines. The third abbot of Cîteaux was an Englishman, Stephen Harding. Under his guidance the numbers of monks grew and new monasteries were started by the monks who were known as Cistercians. They built their monasteries in remote places, away from the possible temptations of town life. Their first English house was at Waverley in Surrey, but their most famous houses were in Yorkshire. Riveaulx (*pic. 69*) was founded in 1132 in an attempt to re-make the area which had been devastated by William in his harrying of the North (page 19). Another famous Yorkshire house was at Fountains (*pics. 70 and 71*).

There were a number of other, smaller orders — the canons of St. Augustine, for example. A young man who wanted to become a monk therefore had a variety of houses and orders to which he could apply. Many hundreds did so: there were about 700 in the community at Fountains in its heyday.

The monastery

When the monks came to Lewes it was at the invitation of William de Warren, the earl of Surrey, who explained that he wanted to

> found some religious houses for our sins and the safety of our souls . . .
> we gave them a church built of stone under the castle at Lewes and as much
> land and beasts and goods as would keep twelve monks there.

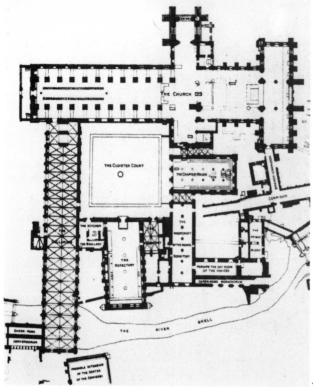

◀ **70**   Ground plan of Fountains Abbey.

71   Fountains Abbey today. The most famous Cistercian monasteries were in Yorkshire, but another famous one is Tintern Abbey.

72   The *lavatorium* at Gloucester. Notice the decorated ceiling — evidence of the fine craftsmanship of medieval monks.

▼

▼

73   The great church, once part of the monastery, now Chester Cathedral. See also *pic. 61*.

74   Worcester Cathedral. You can see the cloisters round the square lawn.

77

Other monasteries were founded on land given by other noblemen, by kings and by princes, all of whom hoped that the monks would pray for them and their families.

All monasteries were built to a similar pattern. *Pic. 70* is a ground plan of Fountains Abbey, and there is an aerial view of the remains of that Abbey in *pic. 71*. Fountains, like most other abbeys, lies in a sheltered valley which meant that the monastery was built alongside a stream, as you can see in the pictures. The stream provided water for the kitchens. Also the monks were able to pipe water from the stream to the *lavatorium* where they washed (*pic. 72*) before going into the chapel or the dining-room. The monks also built toilets which were either drained into or flushed by the stream. This was a luxury that was enjoyed in very few castles or even palaces. Monasteries were healthier as well as holier places.

The cloister

The most important building in the monastery was the great church (*pics. 61 and 73*). Some monastic churches still remain — as cathedrals at Canterbury, Durham and Westminster Abbey, for example. We shall see that the monks spent a good deal of their time in the church.

But if you look at the plan of Fountains (*pic. 70*) you will see that the cloister lay at the heart of the monastic buildings. This was the covered passage-way (*pic. 74*) which led from the church to other parts of the monastery. The passage-way ran in a square round a plot of grass. Each monk had his own seat in the cloister — as you can still see if you visit Westminster Abbey. This was the monk's study and sitting-room, where he read, wrote, studied and heard lectures.

The chapter house

Here the monks met after breakfast each morning. After the reading of a chapter from their rules (hence the name of the room) the head of the monastery (the abbot) gave the orders for the day's work. The chapter house was a sort of monastic office where the monks also made decisions about buying more land, animals or machinery.

Other rooms

You will see that there were many other rooms in the monastery. From the *dorter* (dormitory) where the monks slept there was a staircase down to the church, so that the monks did not have to go out into the night air on their way to the first of the day's services. The *frater* was the dining-room or refectory, where meals were eaten in silence, while the monks listened to a reading from a book about one of the saints. The abbot had his own lodging away from the main buildings, where he could entertain important visitors — who came on behalf of the King, maybe — without disturbing the life of the monks.

In the infirmary the infirmarian would look after any monks who were sick and also provide treatment for people living in the district around the monastery.

The monastery was like a hospital and health centre, as well as a welfare centre for beggars and other poor people.

The warming room

It is worth noting this room, where the monks went to dry out when they came in from a day's work in the fields. There was no central heating system in the cold monastery. It was wise of the planners to provide a room where

75 A page from the Canterbury Psalter, which was written by the scribe Eadwine. This is a picture of Eadwine at Christ Church in Canterbury. Notice his habit (clothing) and the cutting tool and pen he is using. Notice also the highly decorated border to the page.

76 Medieval builders at work. Notice the wheelbarrow and the way in which the men took stone up to upper storeys.

clothes could be dried in front of open fires and where the monks could get some warmth back into their cold bones before going in to pray.

Guest house and lay brothers

There were several areas of a monastery kept for the lay brothers — men who went to live in the monastery without ever becoming priests. They were expected to spend more time in the fields than in the cloisters; to dig rather than to decorate manuscripts (*pic. 75*); to be as much physical as spiritual. They were kept separate from the priest-monks — having their own dining-room, dormitory and infirmary, for if they were sick. This was near the guest house for people who visited the abbey on business.

The monk's work on the land

If they were to keep remote from the outside world, the monks had to be as self-sufficient as possible. That is why William de Warren provided the new monks with "land and beasts and goods". The monks were more educated than most other landowners and their bailiffs. It is not surprising that their lands were more productive than most other farms. The Cistercians became world famous for their skill as sheep farmers which made them rich enough to buy more land to add to that they had been given by their landowning benefactors. So, part of a monk's life was spent at manual work — building the monastery or additions to it (*pic. 76*), ploughing or supervising the work of others, looking after animals, bees, tending to vines and so on.

The monk's praying day

However, the main purpose of the monk's day was to pray and his timetable was arranged around the services he had to attend in the great church. The day began at 2.00 in the morning when the monks went from their dorter to the church for a service of prayers called *Matins* (or morning prayer). This was followed, after a short period for a walk in the cloister, by *Lauds* (or praise). Then they went back to bed until 6.00 a.m. when a service of *Prime* (or first prayers) was followed by a simple mass offered by one of the monks. After Mass and Communion the monks went to the dining-room for breakfast. Then there was the period in the chapter house and study or other work in cloister or field before the bell rang again at about 10.00 a.m. for *Sext* followed by a High Mass celebrated by the abbot. This mass was followed by another service of prayers called *Nones*. The names "*Sext*" and "*Nones*" meant prayers of the sixth hour and the ninth hour after Prime. Originally *Sext* was held at 12.00 a.m., therefore, and *Nones* at 3.00 p.m. but both services came to be held earlier. After *Nones* there was dinner and more work in the field or the cloister until 5.00 p.m. Then *Vespers* (or evening prayers) were held. At about 6.00 p.m. the bell rang again to summon the monks to *Compline*, a service which "completed" the day. After this the monks went

in complete silence to the dormitory where they laid their gowns aside —
until 2.00 a.m. when the day began again.

A novice on his day

Here is a short extract from a letter written by a young man who had just
entered the monastery at Riveaulx:

> Our food is scanty, our garments rough; our drink is from the stream and
> our sleep often upon our book. Under our tired limbs there is but a mat;
> when sleep is sweetest we must rise at a bell's bidding. There is no room for
> self-will because we have to obey; there is no moment for idleness or dissi-
> pation . . .

However, the young man goes on:

> Everywhere peace, everywhere serenity, and a marvellous freedom from the
> tumult of the world. Such unity and concord is there among the brethren
> that each thing seems to belong to us all, and all belongs to each of us . . .

THE YOUNG HISTORIAN

1 As part of the class frieze, paint or draw "The building of our monastery".
 (*Pics. 69-74* and *76* may be some help.)

2 Write the account which might have appeared in newspapers on (i) the
 arrival of the Cistercians at Riveaulx *(pic. 69)*, (ii) the appointment of
 a new abbot, and (iii) the reporter's visit to the cloisters *(pics. 70, 74*
 and *75)*.

3 Make either a model or a sketch plan based on *pic. 70*. Add a brief note
 about each of the main parts of the monastic building.

4 Make an illustrated time-table of a monk's day.

5 Make up short plays on (i) the Cluniacs and William de Warren (page 75),
 (ii) the chapter meeting, (iii) getting up at 2.00 a.m. for prayers, and
 (iv) the warming room on a cold winter's day.

6 Find the names of streets, districts, schools or other places which com-
 memorate the sites of monasteries. There may be some in your locality.
 You might ask your local librarian for help.

7 Paint or draw (i) the *lavatorium (pic. 72)*, (ii) the cloisters *(pics. 74* and *75)*.

8 Write the letter which might have been sent by a villein after a visit to the
 monastery. (He might have written about the number of buildings and
 their size, the beauty of the great church and the cloisters, the water supply
 in *lavatorium* and toilets, the work done by various monks, their fields
 and animals, and so on.)

12 Norman Warfare

77 A battle scene drawn in the latter part of the twelfth century. There had been little change in armour, shields, swords or people's clothing since 1066.

78 A castle besieged by sea and land in 1300. Although after the Norman period, this picture is valuable because it shows how difficult it was for a castle to be overcome. Provided that the people inside had supplies of water and food, they were really safe.

A warlike period

The Norman age began with the Battle of Hastings. One of the best documents on the age is the Bayeux Tapestry which was commissioned by Bishop Odo of Bayeux (*pic. 17*) who had fought in the Battle (page 69).

The age which was born of a battle continued to be warlike. William led his armies into the harrying of the North and the campaigns against Hereward the Wake (page 28). Stephen and Matilda fought a nineteen-year-long civil war over the fields of England. And at the end of the Norman period Englishmen were caught up in the Crusading fervour.

In *pic. 77* you can see a scene which must have been known to many barons, knights and their soldier-followers.

Towns were prepared for war

We have seen that the towns of the Norman period were protected by a surrounding wall (*pics. 42, 43* and *62*). The walls served many purposes; some were connected with trade and the "foreigners" who wanted to sell goods in the towns (page 49). However, a major purpose was to present an obstacle to soldiers of warring barons who might want to loot or plunder the prosperous town. The wall would not keep the soldiers out for long, but it would make their attack a little more difficult and the delay caused would give the townspeople the time to hide away their valuables.

80 Medieval armourers at work on weapons and armour (foreground). On the left is the Roman goddess of Wisdom, Minerva, who is instructing them.
▼

▲
79 King Stephen is shown on this coin in his chain-mail, with his banner and shield.

▲
81 A well-dressed knight of a Crusade, with the banner showing his coat of arms and perhaps, the coat of arms of his overlord.

Castles and warfare

We have already seen that castles were built for protection rather than comfort (page 30), and that the first castles were made quickly, from readily available wood (*pic 12*). However, wooden castles could be burnt down by an enemy who managed to throw flaming torches at the base of the structure. Therefore, in time, stone was used for building castles, which were also built to a greater height and with more protective baileys and moats (*pics. 23, 24 and 26*).

In *pic. 78* you can see a medieval siege. Although it is a siege of 1300 — later than Norman times — it still shows how the people inside the castles had all the advantages — provided that they had an adequate supply of food and water.

During the long civil war, Stephen (*pic. 79*) allowed barons to build more and larger castles. This was the price he had to pay for their support in his struggle against Matilda. Her supporters and Stephen's fought each other, both sides laying siege to the castles of their opponents, but few castles fell to attackers — unless the defenders were starved out or defeated by some fever or disease. The soldiers besieging the castle could always get food by ravaging the surrounding countryside. They trampled over fields, stole animals and raided barns and granaries so that the real sufferers in warfare were the ordinary people.

The blacksmith

Each castle and manor had its blacksmith. He made and repaired tools, put iron rims on cartwheels (*pic. 56*) and produced simple pots (*pics. 51 and 54*), but he was kept busy also making and repairing the weapons used in war (*pic. 80*). There was the sword (*pic. 81*), the lance and the chain-mail dress which was worn by both horseman and horse (*pics. 11, 13, 77-79, 81 and 82*). As time went on, men learned to make ever stronger and more efficient armour. This had to be made by special craftsmen and the local blacksmith was no longer expected to have the skill to do more than repair it when it got damaged.

The Crusades

During the eleventh century there was a revival of religious fervour throughout Europe. This resulted in the founding of new and stricter religious orders (page 75). We have seen too how people went on pilgrimages (page 71). The most important pilgrimage was the one to Jerusalem and the Holy Lands, where Jesus Christ had lived and preached. But the Turks had taken possession of these lands and in 1076 they captured Jerusalem. Stories reached Europe of how the Turks ill-treated pilgrims and in 1095 Pope Urban II called for a Christian army to win back the lands in the East from the Turks. The campaigns against the Turks were called Crusades, the fighters Crusaders. Maybe the most famous English Crusader was Richard I, the Lionheart, who went on the Third Crusade (1189-1192). He was a brother to Henry II, and another of the Plantaganet Kings who followed the Normans on the throne of England.

The feudal army

William had shared the land between his barons, knights and the Church. Each landowner was bound to the King by the Oath at Salisbury (page 23). While a landowner received the privileges of taking payments and services from his feudal inferiors, he also had the duty to provide service to his feudal over-lord (page 18). Each knight had to come to do military service for the King for forty days each year, if called upon to do so. For such service, he had to ride his own horse, have his own armour and weapons and bring with him his own supporters, with their staves, spears or bows and arrows.

82   Once he had been unseated from his horse, the knight was very vulnerable for his heavy armour made it difficult for him to get up again quickly.

The King would also recruit other people to come to fight for him — by offering them money and the promise of rewards if the war was successful. The success of the army depended on the heavily armed knights' getting among the enemy forces, slaying the opposition knights and killing or capturing the leader (*pic. 82*). The infantry who marched in front of the knights had to try to breach the enemy's front lines, so that the knights could get among the enemy. They also had to hold back the enemy from reaching their own leader.

The weakness of the feudal army was that after forty days a knight was free to go home, taking his followers with him. The King hardly had time, therefore, to collect an army to march even against a rebellious baron inside the country. It certainly did not give him long enough if he was planning a foreign war. Henry I (1068-1135) realized this and he introduced a system known as scutage — from the Latin word *"scutum"* meaning shield. Instead of providing the King with knights to do their forty days' service, a baron could pay "shield" money to the King. With this the King could hire soldiers to fight for him without any time limit's being fixed to their service. In this way the King also hoped to make the knights less warlike — and so less of a threat to the Crown.

THE YOUNG HISTORIAN

1   Write an "eye-witness" account of a battle (*pic. 77*). (Read page 16 on the Battle of Hastings. *Pics. 10, 11, 13* and *77-81* will also help you.)
2   Look at *pic. 78*. Write the letter which might have been sent by a soldier taking part in a siege. (He might have written about the lord's armour and his own; pillaging a town and the countryside; the time taken in a siege; death of people — from disease and from wounds received during an attack.)
3   Write the account which might have been given by a child in Norman England after his first visit to the local blacksmith's forge. (*Pic. 80* might help.)
4   Look at *pic. 82*. Why was the unhorsed knight unable to get up? Why was he in danger of death if unhorsed during a battle?
5   As part of the class frieze, paint or draw (i) a coat of arms for a knight, (ii) a Norman shield decorated with a coat of arms.
6   Look at *pic. 81*. Explain why so many people went on Crusades in the eleventh and twelfth centuries. (See also page 84.) What effects did the Crusades have on English trade?
7   Make up short plays about (i) preaching a Crusade, (ii) besieging a town, and (iii) dressing the knight.

13 Entertainment

Riding and fighting

The barons and knights of Norman England spent much of their free time at warlike games, the most exciting and glamorous of which was the tournament. It was introduced into England by the Normans. At first the tournament was a mock battle between two groups of heavily armed knights, each one carrying his decorated shield and wearing his surcoat (or overcoat) with his coat of arms. The two groups charged at each other with lances or swords trying to unhorse an "enemy". As we saw in *pic. 82*, once an armoured knight was unhorsed he was almost helpless. Even in the mock battle of the tournament some knights were badly injured or even killed by the hooves of the heavy warhorses.

Gradually rules were created to make tournaments both safer and more attractive to the public. Special fields, called "lists", were set aside for tournaments. They were ringed around with a high fence to prevent the horses running

◀ 83   Knights fight on foot in a tiltyard, watched by their ladies and, in the foreground, the peasantry. This was an early sort of tournament.

▲
84   Practising with the quintain. You can see the T-shaped quintain, with the shield attached to one end, the bag of sand to the other. The knight drove at the shield with his lance, which made the sandbag swing round and knock him off his horse if he did not ride on quickly enough.

85   Men out hunting — from medieval manuscripts.
▼

off the field. On a tournament day each knight had his own tent or changing room to which his squires and pages (*pics. 17* and *27*) brought his armour (*pics. 11* and *56*), his horse (*pic. 81*), his shields and special clothes for knight and horse. The audience of older knights and ladies sat in specially erected stands. The peasantry were allowed to sit around the outside of the fence to watch their betters at play (*pic. 83*). The master of the tournament would announce the order of the events to be presented.

◄ **86** Men from the lower classes return from a day's hunting — or poaching, perhaps.

87 Inside the great hall at Moat House, Ightone, Kent. This is an artist's attempt to show what life was like in the hall — the window on the right may not really have existed. But you can see the servants kneeling to serve meat from a spit; the dogs waiting for the scraps; the dirty floor (bottom left); signs of success at hunting (the antlers round the walls); and a jester providing entertainment.

▼

Instead of mass battles the rules of the tournament favoured the joust between two knights who charged at each other with lances. The aim was to strike the enemy on his helmet or chest, to unhorse him and so be declared winner. In later medieval times there was a points system — three being awarded for unhorsing an opponent, two for hitting him on the helmet and one for a body blow.

Lower classes and their riding

Jousting was forbidden to anyone below the rank of a squire (page 33), and so younger members of the nobility and freemen invented their own form of sport, using either a quintain or a ring (*pic. 84*). The quintain was a pair of poles arranged in a T-shape. The vertical pole was stuck in the ground. The horizontal one had a shield fixed to one end and a bag of sand at the other. The competitors charged or "tilted" at the shield with a lance. If the shield was hit, the pole swung around and unless the rider was quick the bag of sand would knock him off his horse — to the delight of the crowd and the humiliation of the unhorsed rider.

There was also tilting at a ring, the aim being to run the lance through a ring which was attached to the pole and carry it away. Some people missed the ring altogether, others got their lance stuck too firmly in the ring and had to let go. Only the skilled tilter managed to judge things correctly.

Hunting and hawking

The barons and knights lived in the countryside. It is not surprising that much of their leisure time was spent in country sports. We have seen that hawking was one favourite activity (*pic. 28*).

Hunting (*pic. 85*) was another favourite pastime. In the woods and forests which covered much of the country there were wild boar, wolves, deer and does, foxes and hares to be hunted and caught. The Norman Kings made fierce laws which forbade hunting to anyone owning land worth less than forty shillings a year, but the lower classes went poaching on foot, shot game with bows and arrows and snared rabbits and hares. Like their betters, they regarded their catch as a welcome addition to the diet (*pic. 86*).

The manor and entertainment

We have seen that the people's work in the fields was regulated by the seasons of the year (page 42). The festivals or holy days of the Church were also major landmarks in the year. There were the long holidays at Christmastime, Easter and Whitsuntide, and the hundred or more holidays (or holy days) during the year in honour of Jesus Christ or one of His saints. Also there were traditional holidays of pagan origin, such as May Day and Midsummer's Day.

For many of these holidays the whole village came together. At Christmas, for example, the lord of the manor would often invite his villagers to come to the great hall (*pic. 87*) where the "Lord of Misrule" would be allowed to take charge. This was an attempt to turn things upside down: the lower classes took the place of their betters and the social superiors had to do as they were told. This idea carries on today in the tradition of the armed forces where senior officers serve meals to their men on Christmas Day. There was always a danger that this misrule could spill over into a drunken romp — or worse.

Professional entertainers, particularly minstrels, were in great demand for the various festivals of the year. Bands of minstrels travelled around the country, singing about the saints or the brave deeds of some famous knight. Others sang comic, bawdy songs which pleased the peasantry. Their songs were accompanied by music played on the gitern (guitar), bagpipes, lutes, tambourines and

▲
88 A minstrel with a kind of lute.

89 These scenes of ▶ archery are from a fourteenth-century manuscript, later than Norman times, but they show the butt — the target for the archers' arrows — and the cross bow (top picture) was much the same as it always had been.

90

cymbals (*pic. 88*). Sometimes the minstrels were joined by jugglers, contortionists and rope-walkers, and a kind of circus in which dogs, bears, horses and monkeys did tricks.

These wandering bands of minstrels were also the means by which the people of the countryside heard the latest news — in an age when there were no newspapers or television. Their coming was doubly welcome to the inhabitants of the isolated villages therefore.

The villagers and sport

The barons and knights were rough, warlike men with little education (page 33). Their sport — hunting and hawking — was bloody. Their villagers followed their example in their idea of what was entertainment. For instance, they enjoyed watching bear-baiting (*pic. 65*), wrestling, and competitions to catch a pig by its soaped tail.

There were also frequent competitions in archery — another instance of the link between entertainment and war. The bow was the chief weapon of the common infantry soldiers in battle and lords encouraged their menfolk to keep well practised in using it. Indeed, in some villages and even in some towns there were special places set aside for archery. A butt — a mound of turf — was made and circles were marked on it, for a target (*pic. 89*).

The Church, theatre and the town

A popular form of entertainment were the Miracle Plays. These were put on in churches, particularly at Easter and Christmastime. The priests were the actors who presented a few simple scenes from the life of Christ or from an Old Testament story. Some priests even introduced scenery into their churches. It was St. Francis of Assisi (1182-1226) who built the first Christmas crib, around which actors represented Mary, Joseph, the three kings and the shepherds who came to worship the infant Jesus.

At first these plays were put on inside the churches. But by 1100 some plays wanted larger casts and there was not enough room inside the church, and so the plays moved out into the square in front of the church or, in some cases, to special buildings. When the plays were moved out into the open, the Church decided that priests should not be the actors. Members of the guilds (page 49) began to take part, for example. Since the new actors did not know as much Latin as the priests, the language of the plays also changed and by the end of the Norman period the actors were using the Normanized English that the majority understood (*pic. 90*).

Games

A number of ball games were played in Norman England. There was football — sometimes with one goal in one village and the other goal in another. This meant that the pitch might be three or four miles long and would cut across

91

90   The scene of Jesus before Pilate from the Coventry Miracle Play. Members of guilds took part in the plays.

▲
91   A scene from a twelfth-century manuscript showing a *cryc*. It looks like a hockey stick, but was the ancestor of the modern cricket bat.

fields, streams, ditches and hillsides. There was also cricket of a kind — played with a curved stick or *cryc* (*pic. 91*). In club-ball a player had a straight bat with which to hit the ball. He was out only if someone caught the ball — for there was no wicket. In stool-ball the batsman was out if the ball hit a stool used as a wicket. In trap-ball (*pic. 92*) a ball shot out of a trap and the batter had to hit it as far as he could. He was out if he was caught. In some parts of the country this game was slightly different: the aim was to hit the ball the greatest distance.

Other popular games were quoits, bowls, skittles — the forerunner of pinball. Adults played games which today are children's games — blind man's buff (known as Hoodman Blind), Leap Frog and chasing games which are still played in school playgrounds under various names such as "He" or "It".

Indoor games — chess, draughts and dice — were more common in the homes of the rich than in the hovels of the peasants. Such games required the room and peace which was rarely available in the cruck house and not always present in the simpler manor hall. The Normans would have welcomed homes like ours, where different members of the family may "do their own thing" in one of various rooms or where everyone may join together, if they wish, to watch television. On the other hand, we would find it very strange if we were transported from the twentieth century back into Norman England and had to live in one of the small villages of the period. The Norman period was hardly "the good old days".

THE YOUNG HISTORIAN

1   Look at *pics. 85* and *86*. Give an account of a day's hunting by (i) the lord, (ii) his squire, and (iii) a villein.
2   Write the newspaper account which might have appeared about "The Lord of Misrule" (pages 89-90 and *pic. 87*).
3   Look at *pic. 90*. Why were the early dramas called "Miracle Plays"? Why, at first, were they put on inside the churches? Suggest three titles which might have been used. Make an illustration advertizing one of these plays.
4   Make a poster advertizing either a tournament or a fair.
5   As part of the class frieze, paint or draw (i) the lists (page 87), (ii) an archery competition (*pic. 89*), (iii) medieval musicians (*pic. 88*).
6   Make up a short play on each of the following: (i) the squire learning to joust, (ii) tilting at the quintain (*pic. 84*), (iii) any one of the ball games mentioned in the text (pages 91-2).

◀   **92**   Trap-ball.

Other Visual Aids

16 mm Films

The Bayeux Tapestry	E.F.V.A.
Medieval England	Gateway
Life in a Medieval Town	Gateway
The Medieval Village	Rank
The Medieval Monastery	Rank
The Medieval Village	Rank
The Three Field System	Gateway

35 mm Filmstrips

The Norman Conquest	Visual Information Services
William the Conqueror	Rank
William II	Rank
Henry I	Rank
Stephen	Rank
Henry II	Rank
William the Conqueror	Wills and Hepworth
Hugh the Norman Page	Hulton
The Bayeux Tapestry	Rank
The Bayeux Tapestry	Visual Publications
The Invasion and Conquest of England	Visual Publications
The Monastery	Common Ground

Index

The numbers in **bold** type refer to pages on which illustrations appear

abbots, 22, 69, 75, 78, 80
aldermen, 51-2
ale, 32, 36, 39, 44, 58, 62
Alfred, King, 47
Anglo-Saxons, the, 9, 18, 47, 61, 64, **11**
animals, 11, 43, 44
Anjou, 26-7
Anselm, Archbishop, 71
apprentices, 49, **50**, 62
Aquitaine, 26-7
archbishops, 22, 69-71
archery, 91, **90**
armour, 15, 33, 88, **14, 15, 82, 83, 85**
army, English, 28
  feudal, 26, 85-6
  Norman, 14
  Saxon, 13-15, **15**
arrows, 85, **90**
Atheling, Edgar, 16
Augustine, St. 75

bailey, the, 30, 84, **29**
bailiff, the 36, 42, 49, 80
barn, **37**
barons, 17-18, 20, 22-4, 26-7, 30, 36, 54, 83-4, 87, 89
  and castles, 28-34
  clothing, 59
  in council, 20
  and law, 25
bathing, 38, **38**
Bayeux Tapestry, the, 7, 13, 69, 83, **7, 8, 11, 13, 14, 15, 21, 55, 57, 61**
bear-baiting, 91
Beckett, Thomas à, 70-1, **73**
beds, 31-2, 54, **31**
Benedictines, the, 75
bishops, 22, 67-9, 71
blacksmiths, 38, 62, 84
boats, 62, **61**
boon work, 9, 41, 43
boroughs, 47, 64
Bosham, **8**
bows, 85, **90**
bread, 58
Bristol, 48
builders, **79** (see also masons)
burgesses, 47, 49, 51-2
Bury St. Edmunds, 71

Cambridge, 30
Canterbury, **69**
  Archbishop of, 8, 26, 69-71, **73**

Cathedral, 78, **61, 79**
carpenters, 51, 64, **50**
carts, 62, 64, **61**
castles, 8, 15, 18-20, 26-28, 30-31, 47, 84, **14, 29, 31, 82**
  life in, 30-34
cathedrals, 67-8, 78, **61, 77**
Celts, the, 9, 18
chain-mail, **14, 83, 84**
Cheshire, 19
Chester, 18, 47, 49, **77**
children, 40, 93, **44, 92**
China, 66
Christmas, 89-91
Church, the, 67-73
  Courts, 70-1
  in England, 8, 70
  festivals, 39-40, 89-91
  as landowners, 17, 55-6, 38-9, 71
  Norman, 7, 68, **11**
  Saxon, 67-8, **8, 11**
  schools, 70
  village, 10, 67
Cistercians, the, 75, 80, **74, 76**
Cîteaux, 75
civil war, 26-7, 34, 83
clerks, 36, 70
cloister, 78, **76**
cloth, **44**
clothes, 32, 38, 51, 58, 64, **37, 79, 82**
Cluniacs, the, 75
common, the, 11, 22, 36, 40, **35**
cooking, 58, **38, 57, 59,**
Cornwall, 67
coronation, 17, 30, **11, 13**
cottars, 41-2
courts, baronial, 25
  Church, 70-1
  King's, 25, 36
  manor, 36
craftsmen, 47, 49, 51, 58, 63-4, 71, **62**, 72 (see also guilds)
cricket, 93, **92**
Crown, power of, 25-7 (see also monarchy)
Crusades, the, 66, 83-4, **83**
cups, 32
cutlery, 32, 51, 64, **21, 26, 32**

Danelaw, the, 9, 42
Danes, the, 9, 19, 42, 47, 71

death rates, 40, 51
Devon, 67
dioceses, 67, **74**
diseases, 32, 40, 51, **52**
dishes, 32, 38, 54, **32**
Domesday Book, 19, 22-23, 47, **23**
Dover, 30
drink, 32 (see also ale; wine)
Durham, 8, 19, 78

Easter, 62, 89, 91
eating, 32, 58, **21, 26**
  (see also cups; food; drink; dishes; cutlery)
Edgar Atheling, 16
Edith, Queen, 7
Edward the Confessor, 7, 12-13, 20, 22, **7, 11**
Edwin of Mercia, 19
Eleanor of Aquitaine, 26
entertainers, 39, 71, 87-93
epidemics, 51
Ethelred the Unready, 7

fairs, 47, 49
falconry, 33-4
farming, 9-10, 36, 40-6, **74**
  the year's work, 42-5
Fenland, 28, 48
feudal army, 26, 85-6
  followers, 20, 24, 85
  oath, 23-4, 71
  system, 9-11, 18, 24, 42, 85
fields, open, 10, 54, 58, 63, **10, 41**
fires, 32, 56, 58, **55, 59**
fish, 40, 51, 62, **39, 50, 61**
fishing, 62, **39, 61**
floor covering, 31-2, 38, 88
food, 32-3, 36, 38-40, 42, 46, 58, 70, **21, 26, 57** (see also meat)
  rents, 20, 36
football, 91-3
forests, 36
  royal, 20, 33, **21**
Fountains Abbey, 75, 78, **76**
France, 21, 48, 62, **7**
Francis of Assisi, St., 91
freemen, 41-3, 67
fruit, 40, 43
furniture, 38, 64

games, 91-3
Gloucester, 20, 62, 63, 76
Godwin, Earl, 7-8, 12
government, King's, 23
guilds, craftsmen's, 49, 51, 59, 91, **50, 92**
  merchants', 49, **50**

hall, the, in castle, 31-2, **56**
  in manor, 38, 56, 90, **37, 88**
Halley's Comet, 13, **13**
Harding, Stephen, 75
Hardrada, Harold, 13, **14**
Harold, King, 8, 12-16, **7, 8, 11, 13, 15, 55**
harrying of the North, 19, 28, 75, 83
harvests, 40-1, 43-4, **45**
Hastings, 13-19, 20, 28, 30, 83, **14, 15**
hawking, 33-4, 89, 91, **33**
haymaking, 36, 43, **44**
Henry I, 25, 27, 34, 71, 86, **25**
  II, 27, 34, 71, 84
Hereford, 18
Hereward the Wake, 28, 83
home life, 54-9 (see also castles; houses; manor; women)
houses, cruck, 54-6, **54, 55**
  manor, 10, 36, 54, **35** (see also hall)
  merchants', 57
  royal 20, **21**
  town, 58
Humber, River, 9
hunting, 32-3, 89, 91, **87, 88**

India, 66
Innocent, Pope, 26
Ipswich, 9
iron, 62

Jerusalem, 84
jesters, **88**
journeymen, 50, **62**
joust, 89
Judges, King's, 25, 71, **24**
jury system, the, 27

keep, the, 30, **29**
Kent, 9
King, the advisers to, 20, 22-5, 69

castles of, 21
coronation of, 17, 30, **11, 13,**
and Council, 20, **8**
Courts, 20, 22, 36, 71
estates of, 20
forests of, **21**
funeral of, **11**
ministers of, 9, **8**
officials of, 22
palace of, **7**
power of, 25, 34 (see also crown and monarchy)
travel of, 20
treasury of, 16, 20, 22
King's Lynn, 48
knights, (see also manor)
clothing, 59
dress, 15, 33, 87, **14, 15, 83, 85, 87** (see also armour; chain-mail; lance; shield; sword; weapons)
duties, 18, 85 (see also feudal system)
land of, 22
as landowners, 36
as overlords, 23-4, **35**
training of, 33, 87 (see also pages; squires)
knives, 32 (see also cutlery)

lance, the, 33, 84, 87, 89
landowners, 17-20, 32, 35, 41, 61, 69-71, 80, 85
Laxton, 11, **10**
Lent, 40, 62
leprosy, 40
Lewes, 75
Lincoln, 9, 30, 47, 58, 57
lists, the, 87
London, 8, 9, 13, 16, 17, 20, 30, 48-9, 51, 63-4, 66, **13, 16, 48, 65,**
Tower of, 17, 20, 30, **16, 28**
longships, 13, 15, **14**

Manchester, 47
manor, the, **35**
church, 36, **35**
court, 36
explanation of, 35-6, 42, 45
hall in, 38, 56, 90, **37, 88**
house, 10, 36-8, 89, **35**
income of, 36
life in, 38-40, 49, 54, (see also meals)
lords of, 41, 89-90
officials, 36, 45
stream, 62, **39**
markets, 47, 49, 51-2, 64, **63, 65**
masons, 51, **50** (see also builders)
mayor, the, 52
meals, 31-2, 58 (see also cutlery; dishes; eating; food; tables)
meat, 32, 36, 39-40, 51, 58, 62, **88**

merchants, 47, 49, 58, 71 (see also guilds)
miller, the, 39, 45-6
ministers, the King's, 9, **8**
minstrels, 39, 90, **90**
Miracle Plays, 91, **92**
moat, the, 30, 84, **29**
monarchy, stronger, 20 (see also crown; King)
monasteries, 8, 47, 67-8, 70, 74-81, **74, 76, 77**
money, 62-3
monks, 67, 74-81
Morcar, Earl, 19
motte, 30, **14**

Norfolk, **28**
Norman, abbots, 8
advisers, 8
armour, 15, **14, 15,**
army, 14
barons, 17, 20, 30, 54 (see also barons)
buildings, 7, **8, 11**
castles, 8, 15, 18-19, 30, **14** (see also castles)
cathedrals, 19 (see also cathedrals)
landowners, 17, 19
language, 7
people, 7
ships, 13, **14**
Normandy, 7, 12, 14-15
Duke of, 7
William of, 7, 11-16, 20, 47, 70, **11, 13**
North, the harrying of, 19, 28, 75, 83
Northumberland, 8, 19
Norway, 13-14, 48
Norwich, 9, 49, 67, **48**

oath-taking, 12, 23-4, 71, 85, **11, 24**
Odo of Bayeux, 69, 83, **21**
Offa's Dyke, 18, **17**
open fields, 10, 36, 42, 44, **10, 35, 41** (see also commons; farming; fields; strips)
orders, religious, 75, 84
Benedictines, 75
Canons of St. Augustine, 75
Cistercians, 75, 80, **74, 76**
Cluniacs, 75
overlords, 49, **35**
oxen, **9**
Oxford, 9, 48

pages, 33, 88
Parliament, 22
peasants, 88, **37, 87**
pedlars, 39
Pembroke Castle, 30, 47, **29**
Pevensey Bay, 15
pilgrimages, 70-1, 73, 84, **73**
plagues, 51
Plantaganets, the, 26-7, 71, 84
ploughs, 11, 36, **9, 35, 41**
poaching, 89, **88**

Pope, the, 26, 70, 84
population, size of, 9
town, 64, 67
ports, 48, **48**
pots, 58, 62, 84, **38, 59**
priests, 22, 34, 67, 71
punishments, 25

quintain, the, 89, **87**

reeve, the, 36, 42, 49, **37, 45**
religion, 24 (see also church; monasteries)
religious orders, 75
rents-in-kind, 9, 20, 23, 36, 42, 62
Richard I, 84
riding, 87
Riveaulx, 75, **74**
roads, 20, 62, **61**
roofs, 56, 68
rushes (for floors), 31-32, 43, 56

Salisbury, Oath at, 23-4, 85, **8**
Saxon, army, 13-15, **15**
bishops, 16
churches, 67-8, **8, 11**
landowners, 19
nobles, 7-9, 16-17
and Normans, 16, **14**
towns, 47
schools, 70
Scotland, 8, 22
scurvy, 40
scutage, 86
serfs, 41-2
servants, 33, 70, **57, 88**
sheep, 43, 59, 80, **44**
sheriffs, 23
shields, 15, 33, 86-9, **15, 82, 83, 87**
ships, 13, 15, 28, **14**
shops, 49, 63-4, **62**
Shrewsbury, 18
sickles, 37
sieges, 84, **82**
silk, 61, 66
slaves, 41-2
Spain, 62
spices, 61, 66
spinning-wheel, the, 59
sport, 91-3
squires, 33, 88-9
Stamford Bridge, 13-15
standard of living, 54, 71
Stephen, King, 25-7, 83-4, **83**
stewards, 36
streams, 62, **39**
streets, 49, 51, 62, 64
strip-farming, 10, 36, 42, 62, **10, 35, 41**
swords, 15, 33, 84, 87, **14, 82**

tables, 62, **21**
taxes, 23, 45
tenants, 20, 23, 62
Thames, River, 9, 16, 48, **16**
theatre, 91, **92**
thegn, 9, 13, 16-18, 36
Thetford, 9

Tintern Abbey, **76**
tithes, 67
tolls, 47, 49, 52, 64, **65**
tools, 39, 62, 84, **14, 35, 79**
tournaments, 33, 87, 88-89, **87**
Tower of London, 17, 20, 30, **16, 28**
towns, 13, 46-52, 61-2, 64, 67, 70
gates of, 47, 49, 52, 64, **48**
government of, 49, 51-2
populations of 64
streets, in, 49, 51, 62, 64
walls of, 49, 51-2, 64, **83, 48**
trade, foreign, 47-9, 61-6
inland, 61-6
traders, 47
travel, 20, **61**
trial by ordeal, 27

vegetables, 40, 43, 58
Vikings, the, 13-15, 47, **14**
villages, 9-10, 13, 16, 19, 22, 36, 40, 51, 54, 59, 61, 64
villeins, 41-2, 49, 67

wages, 50
Wales, 18, 22, 30, **17**
Wallingford, 16, 26
war, civil, 26-7, 34, 83
warfare, 82-6 (see also sieges)
water supply, 51, 84, 52, 82
Watling Street, 9
Waverley, 75
weapons, 16, 33, 62, 84, **83** (see also armour; chain-mail; shields; swords)
Westminster, 12, 17, 20, 78, **7, 8**
White Tower, the, 20, **16**
William of Normandy, 7, 11-16, 20, 47, 70, **11, 13**
the Conqueror, 17-18, 28, 30, 35, 70, **16, 21**
King, 17-20, 23-4, 27, 71, 75, **21**
and the monarchy, 20
William Rufus, 24-5, 34
Winchester, 16, 20, **8**
windows, 38, 54, 58, **31, 88**
wine, 32, 43, 48, 61-2, **61**
Witan, the, 9, 12-13, **8**
women, 38, 59, **44**
wool, 38, 47-8, 59, **44, 59, 61**
Worcester, 76
workers, 59 (see also craftsmen)
wrestling, 91

yeomen, 34
York, 9, 30, 49, 63, 69, 70
Yorkshire, 19, 75, **74, 76**